D0316627

Education Policy, Practice and the Professional

LEEDS TRINITY LIBRARY

299871 4

Also available from Continuum

The Study of Education: An Introduction, Jane Bates and Sue Lewis

Teaching and Learning and the Curriculum, Emmanuel Mufti and Mark Peace

Educational Equality, Harry Brighouse, James Tooley and Kenneth R. Howe, edited by Graham Haydon

Special Educational Needs: A New Look, Mary Warnock and Brahm Norwich, edited by Lorella Terzi

Teaching Thinking Skills, Stephen Johnson and Harvey Siegel, edited by Christopher Winch

Education Policy, Practice and the Professional

Jane Bates,
Sue Lewis and
Andy Pickard

continuum

379.41
BAT

LEEDS TRINITY UNIVERSITY COLLEGE

Continuum International Publishing Group

The Tower Building   80 Maiden Lane
11 York Road   Suite 704
London SE1 7NX   New York NY 10038

www.continuumbooks.com

© Jane Bates, Sue Lewis and Andy Pickard 2011

All rights reserved. No part of this publication may be reproduced or transmitted in any form or by any means, electronic or mechanical, including photocopying, recording, or any information storage or retrieval system, without prior permission in writing from the publishers.

Jane Bates, Sue Lewis and Andy Pickard have asserted their right under the Copyright, Designs and Patents Act, 1988, to be identified as Authors of this work.

British Library Cataloguing-in-Publication Data
A catalogue record for this book is available from the British Library.

ISBN: 978-0-8264-9977-6 (paperback)
        978-1-4411-1520-1 (hardcover)

Library of Congress Cataloging-in-Publication Data
Bates, Jane (Jane E.)
Education policy, practice and the professional / Jane Bates, Sue Lewis and Andy Pickard.
p. cm.
Includes bibliographical references and index.
ISBN: 978-0-8264-9977-6
1. Educational equalization–Great Britain. 2. Working class–Education–Great Britain.
3. Public schools–Great Britain. 4. Education and state–Great Britain. 5. Teachers–
Professional relationships–Great Britain. I. Lewis, Sue (Sue E.) II. Pickard, Andy, 1947–
III. Title.

LC213.3.G7B38 2011
379.41–dc22

2010043686

Typeset by Newgen Imaging Systems Pvt Ltd, Chennai, India
Printed and bound in Great Britain

To Trevor, Albert and Celia
For another ruined summer!

Our thanks also go to Angela Harnett
for her contribution to the Chapter on Schools.

Contents

List of Figures and Tables

Figures

Tables

Foreword

In this book we set out to explore the links between the beginnings of state education and teacher professionalism and the challenges faced by the education community since the 'Thatcher' years. Our initial focus, therefore, is the state's first interventions in education. This is then followed by an examination of the contemporary policy context, in particular the education policies developed by New Labour.

The book has been written for our students, undergraduates working toward an Education Studies degree, and as such it presents alternative ways of understanding the relationships between education policy formation and the wider social context. We have chosen to focus only on selected aspects of historical policy making, because they have a degree of resonance with contemporary themes. We want our students to understand the ways in which education policy was first conceived and the processes that the policy makers followed. We also want them to be able to recognize the origins of contemporary debates and to realize that the questions being asked now are not dissimilar to those being grappled with more than a century earlier.

The historical detail of Chapters 1 and 2 allows us the opportunity to deconstruct the language used by the policy makers responsible for the beginnings of state education, in England in particular. Such people had enormous influence over the shape of the system in which we, as teachers and educators, have been working. We are now at a point in history where education is about to undergo major change and it is possible that we are witnessing the end of the process that is described in Part I.

In Part II of the book, we examine contemporary themes in education, but through a different lens, as we are as yet denied the retrospective lens of history. Throughout, special reference is made to schools and teachers and what is perceived as policy hysteria or policy faddism. We also reflect on the possible direction that education policy and teacher professionalism may take in the future. Specific issues are highlighted under 'Focus' areas, to enable the student reader to fully appreciate both the historical and the contemporary policy context. We consider this to be a true introduction to education policy.

A key motif of the book is the idea of a policy cycle – economic and social crises result in a change in education policy. Initially, the new policies impact positively on teacher professionalism; later, however, perceived policy failure has an adverse effect on teachers' reputations. Particular themes that we felt worthy of consideration include:

- The role played by social class and government responses to an increasingly vocal working class
- The emergence of teaching as a profession and their conditions of service
- Patterns of change/reform/challenge
- The notion of payment by results and its relationship to assessment

- Major questions around the curriculum – which subjects are central?
- Funding arrangements – who should pay and how much?
- The emergence of the global economy and the perceived centrality of an educated workforce
- The development of the primary and secondary systems and the formation of a diversity of schools
- The big question of who should control the education system – the government, local authorities, parents, teachers?
- The influence of the church and individual philanthropists
- Variable attitudes towards teachers – the emergence of first government and then public mistrust
- Changing notions of teacher professionalism.

We hope that, overall, the book will provide students with an accessible account of where we came from, where we are and where we might be going. We hope you enjoy 'the journey'!

Part I
Historical Perspectives

Policy Dawn 1837–1889

The Rise of Elementary Schooling and Teacher Professionalism

Chapter Outline

Introduction

The process of educational policy making, implementation and review is complex. At the policy-making stage key questions include:

- Who is involved in creating a particular policy?
- Does the language of a policy or policies reveal the assumptions, motivation and values of its originators?
- Does the policy have stated intentions and envisaged outcomes?
- How do the policy makers envisage their policy being implemented?

As educational policies are implemented they present a further set of questions:

- In what forms and with what manifestations does policy implementation occur?
- Are the meanings of these manifestations clear to all those responsible for implementation or are they ambiguous and contested?
- Does the implementation create further difficulties and dilemmas?
- Do those who are responsible for implementation acknowledge the value of a policy and assimilate it; or do they adapt it in ways which are different from the policy makers' intentions; or are they indifferent or even resistant to its implementation?

And then almost invariably sooner or later policies are reviewed. This may happen in a formal sense: for example, as we shall see, it was nineteenth-century practice to sometimes review the implementation and operation of major educational policies by Royal Commission. More often policies are reviewed informally, being seen as inadequate to meet new needs as they arise. Again, policy review creates its own questions:

- Who has benefited from the implementation of a policy and how?
- What counts as success or failure?
- Have the intentions of the policy makers been met?
- Has a policy had unintended consequences?
- How are any unintended consequences explained and understood?

All of these policy-making, implementation and review questions challenged those responsible for making nineteenth-century policy as much as they do their successors today. History, however, adds its own special twist to trying to understand events in what has become a distant past. Historical contexts are not those of contemporary policy making. The historian, therefore, will attempt to describe what they think is the backdrop to the events they are describing. Inevitably, such descriptions are selective and shaped by the historian's own preoccupations: they are never that 'will of the wisp' – 'objective'. Yet they do have the great merit of drawing attention to the ways in which policies can never be divorced from the societies in which they sit.

The Historical Context: The Importance of Social Class

Social policy, such as that to do with education, does not happen in a vacuum: it is intimately linked to economic, social and political events. This chapter shows how the social history of the nineteenth century shaped educational policies of the time and affected the emerging teaching profession. In so doing, this chapter and those that follow, lie firmly in a tradition of writing about the history of education pioneered by A. E. Dobbs (1919) almost a century ago when he argued that progress in English education owed less to the zeal of its advocates than to changes in social structure with often no apparent connection with educational movements. The chapter is concerned with elementary schooling because that was the central preoccupation of the policy makers of the time. For much of the century, formal education for most children was an intermittent affair and largely over by the age of 12 years at the very latest. Schools were elementary rather than, in our modern terminology, 'primary' simply because higher, or secondary, education was restricted to a very small minority of children. Dobbs defined the elementary school as

> a specialised instrument of training and instruction necessitated by industrial developments, which, dissolving the older forms of life, opened access to a more complex existence along a path beset

with difficulties and requiring a higher degree of mental equipment than had sufficed in earlier times. (1919, p. viii)

This may be overly simple for modern scholarship, and the condescension to the past implicit in the phrase 'a higher degree of mental equipment' certainly grates, but as a positional starting point for what follows, it has considerable merit.

Historians deal in dates. In other words their stock in trade is to attach particular significance to particular years. What counts as a significant year depends on the kind of history they are writing. It may be the coronation or death of a monarch, the outbreak of a major war or the peace treaty that brings a war to an end, or it may be an economic disaster such as a world slump. The chapter bookends here are located in years of industrial and political debate in order to underline the intimate embrace between educational policy and the experiences of social crisis.

Chartism

Why then 1837? In the two generations from the 1790s until the 1830s, British society underwent possibly the most rapid economic and social change in its history. It became neither fully urbanized nor fully industrialized (that happened in the second half of the century), but pre-industrial work patterns and their associated cultural formations were broken up. The heart of the earlier economy lay with the artisan trades, which were groups of men and women possessing particular skills and their own tools who retained considerable control over when and where they worked and when they relaxed and played. Population growth and economic difficulties made it impossible for many of these skilled tradespeople and the artisan trades societies into which they were organized to retain their old authority and independence.

The experience of rapid change led inevitably to a demand for political change which was deep seated enough to begin to redefine the relationship between the English state and its people. At the time, the state was profoundly undemocratic as we would understand democracy today. Few men and no women were entitled to vote in parliamentary elections. Day-to-day government still remained to a remarkable extent (to our eyes) in the hands of the monarch and his or her advisers in the Privy Council. The House of Lords remained hugely powerful and the major way in which 'citizens' sought to influence politics was by petitioning parliament or taking their protests on to the streets, or both.

By the 1790s, such old certainties were breaking down. The American War of Independence and the French Revolution combined with home-grown radicalism to let a different kind of democratic genie out of the bottle. For radicals, democracy was the entitlement of our shared humanity, rather than being vested in property ownership, and they promoted this idea through a myriad of pamphlets, radical newspapers and speeches to sometimes vast popular gatherings. Harried and repressed by an aristocratic state which could not countenance such a fundamental redefinition of democracy, it was nevertheless an idea which refused to die.

In 1837, these radical ideas crystallized around the *Charter*. Chartism was a diverse and diffuse movement with each locality having its own distinctive characteristics. However, the central features of Chartism included a working-class national leadership, a mass national participation, extensive means of promoting its ideas through radical newspapers and local and national meetings and, above all, a national political agenda on the six points of the Charter. They were:

- universal manhood suffrage
- a secret ballot
- annual parliaments
- payment of members of parliament
- constituencies of equal size
- abolition of the property qualification for MPs.

The response of the state was entirely predictable. Troops were used to suppress Chartist demonstrations and ringleaders were imprisoned, transported or occasionally hung. By 1840, it was becoming clear to some Chartist leaders that the government was unlikely to concede directly to their demands, and some began to advocate what has been termed 'knowledge Chartism', that is, the building of Chartist schools and other means of spreading radical ideas to ensure that the new ideas around democracy took root for future generations.

In 1848, popular political Chartism held its last hurrah with a meeting of some 50,000 to 100,000 people on Kennington Common near London. A petition with five million signatures (although possibly only two million were genuine) was presented to parliament and totally ignored. Activity continued throughout the summer but by the end of the year it was clear that Chartism as a mass movement was over, although not the democratic ideal it had fostered.

Why is radicalism generally and Chartism in particular so central to our understanding of educational policy making in the period? The answer to this question lies in the role education plays in society and politics. Just as individuals sometimes see education as a way of fostering their well-being, modern governments invest in education in order to achieve progress, as they see it, for a society as a whole. This was not a point of view to which English governments subscribed before the 1830s, but the Chartists did. They built on working-class traditions of self-education to redefine the role of education broadly and to help bring about the transformation of the relationship between the state and its citizens into a democratic form.

The presence of these self-generated working-class forms of education are now well documented by historians. John Harrison's (1963) early work on adult education was followed by further studies including that by Thomas Laqueur (1976) which even reclaimed the Sunday school as essentially a working-class creation. Thus it becomes problematic to see state educational policy as simple altruism: to some extent state interest in elementary schooling in the 1830s and 1840s was a policy of replacing emergent popular educational institutions with those that policy makers found more congenial. As we shall see this is not an unfamiliar story in the history of educational policy making.

The Strike

If 1837, the year of the Charter, is now explained as the appropriate beginning for this chapter, why does it close in 1889? The 'defeat' of Chartism was followed by a decade of relative social quiescence variously described as the age of consensus, the high Victorian years or the age of equipoise. There were still moments of local working-class protest, some of it highly organized, and the upper and middle classes continued to be exercised by the pernicious effects, as they saw it, of poverty, but there was no mass challenge to the legitimacy of the aristocratic state.

By the 1860s, agitation for an extension of male suffrage reappeared and there was a limited extension of the franchise in 1867, although the right to vote was still tied to property. By the 1870s, women, too, were beginning to agitate for political rights, but it was the onset of a major economic depression in the 1870s which lasted for 20 years and which renewed radicalism. Of course, the world of the 1880s was very different from that of the 1830s. In place of a largely rural population with scattered towns and occasional large cities, England was now thoroughly urbanized. Eighty per cent of the population was now ubiquitously categorized as 'working class' and they, together with a vast army of lower-middle-class clerks serving the rapidly expanding commercial enterprises, dominated the late Victorian cities. There was also a renewed popular appetite for discussion of all kinds of ideas, scientific, religious and philosophical, as well as political. Socialist societies in a number of forms appeared to question the current social, economic and political arrangements of contemporary society. The renewal of radical ideas and economic depression came together quite startlingly in 1889 in the Great Dock Strike.

The strike was the single most important event in labour history in the second half of the nineteenth century. At the time, London was the greatest port in the world with ships from all over the world loading and unloading goods to meet the insatiable needs of British industrial, commercial and imperial power. All of this activity was serviced by an army of casual workers who were employed on a daily or even hourly basis as was required and then laid off as the docks became idle. By 1889, some of these men, aided and abetted by representatives from skilled unions, had organized themselves into the Dockers' Union. In June they struck, demanding sixpence per hour – the Dockers' 'silver orb'. The strike was long and bitter and after 6 weeks it looked as if the men might be forced back to work. Their cause was rescued by sympathetic unions in Australia who sent £30,000 in gold for the union coffers. It was enough: the dock owners capitulated to union demands. Symbolically the strike was very important. The alliance of skilled and unskilled workers was achieved in the face of the huge fissure between those whose skills could promise regular employment and the casual poor whose lives were ones of continual struggle and uncertainty.

The relationship between all of this and educational policy making remains to be explored, but in very general terms, an educational system created around the belief that its users came from dissolute and possibly revolutionary homes would no longer serve, as policy makers contemplated the arrival of the twentieth century. A mature working class busy creating trades unions and independent political agencies required different kinds of educational policies.

Policy Dawn: Elementary Education and Teacher Professionalism

This chapter has argued thus far that educational policies cannot be understood if divorced from their historical context and that the most important political contextual feature of the nineteenth century was the emergence of the working class. This is not to say that education was not profoundly influenced by other agencies. The churches and their denominational rivalries were clearly central to the building and maintenance of the schools and the shaping of the curriculum. The responses of the children who attended elementary schools and the parents who sent them there helped to determine the quality of education. Educational policy, however, has a narrower focus. It is produced by politicians, administrators and those who seek to influence them with the purpose of shaping future society. It is therefore about what ends matter most at the time and the means deemed best suited to achieve these ends. This section therefore examines the motivations of those most active in mid-nineteenth-century policy making and the policy outcomes of their endeavours.

Educational policy making really begins in 1839. Prior to that, the state restricted its activities to episodic efforts to support the work of the religious societies who were building schools for working-class children. By 1839 this support took the form of an annual parliamentary grant. However, by 1839 it was also becoming clear that an administrative system was required to oversee this expenditure. Modern cabinet government, whereby the Prime Minister chairs meetings of the great ministers of state, had yet to emerge. Instead, executive government remained in the hands of the Privy Council who constitutionally had the job of advising the monarch in the running of the nation's affairs. Education required running, and so the Committee of the Privy Council on Education was set up to do the job.

The first secretary to the new committee was James Kay Shuttleworth. As plain Dr James Kay, he had written an influential report in 1834 on the poor of Manchester. An enthusiastic believer in the power of the state to assist those in civil society active in social reform, Kay Shuttleworth's first task was to appoint two men to the new post of Her Majesty's Inspectors (HMI) of Schools. Their role was to inspect schools in receipt of government grants and then to present their findings in an annual report to the Education Committee. Neither of the first two appointments was a conspicuous success. Hugh Tremenheere, who inspected non-conformist schools, so outraged the school managers that he had to be moved to inspecting mines where it was felt he could do less damage. John Allen, his Anglican counterpart, regarded himself as a clergyman first and civil servant second. He insisted on sending his annual report to the Archbishop of Canterbury from whom Kay Shuttleworth had to retrieve it. Despite these early setbacks, the number of HMIs increased steadily through the 1840s and in effect, while continuing to insist on their quasi-independent status, became the major means by which government influenced educational practice for the next 150 years.

By 1840, therefore, educational policy making had delivered two essential principles which were to stand the test of time: the state had a role in funding educational provision and a duty to ensure that this money was well spent. Both of these principles have been a source of policy conflict ever since. The first raises the issue of to what extent and to whom should the money go. The second leads to the question of what counts as good spending.

Having established an administrative system and means of policing standards, Kay Shuttleworth turned his attention to the problem of teacher supply. It is a truism that schools are only as good as the teachers who work in them, but at least in the modern era we have a plethora of information about the success or otherwise of teachers. We know very little about nineteenth-century teachers and still less about those who lived their lives before the policy initiatives of the 1840s. Nevertheless, we know that there was a felt need among educational policy makers to ensure that the expanding elementary schools needed to be taught by properly trained teachers.

Policy at the time was expressed and promoted through the annual minutes of the Education Committee. The minutes for 1846 are the most ambitious of the decade and quite possibly the most ambitious, far-reaching piece of policy making in the history of English education. They guaranteed funds being available to school managers to build and to equip schools, to supply those schools with professionally trained and relatively well paid teachers and to augment school income with regular funding from the state. In return the school managers would have to agree to their schools being inspected by HMIs with satisfactory outcomes.

Thus, schools from 1846 could apply for a grant to help them build a school. They could then apply for book grants, blackboard grants and slate grants to equip their new building. From 1853, after a protracted parliamentary debate on how many days a child could be expected to attend school, attendance grants could also be claimed. The 1846 minutes also enabled schools to appoint a pupil teacher, a young person of 13 or so years of age who would work in the school learning to be a teacher. The pupil teacher would receive a very modest salary (up to £10 per year) and the school would receive a pupil teacher grant. The really talented or well-placed future teachers could apply for a 'Queen's scholarship' to attend one of the newly opened teacher training colleges from which they would obtain, if successful, a teacher's certificate. These certificated teachers would be entitled to augment their salaries with additional government payments in line with the value of their certificates. Thus, a first-class certificated teacher could look forward to receiving an annual £30 postal order – a decent sum at a time when teacher salaries could be as little as £25 per year. Teachers were even promised pensions at the end of their teaching careers.

These remarkable 1846 minutes dominated the administration of education for the next 25 years. The state had not yet created a state-run educational system – the Protestant and increasingly the Roman Catholic churches remained the most important builders of schools, and the two or three pence per week charged to parents helped to fund their children's education. Nevertheless, the state had established a formidable policy presence in elementary education. Not the least effect of the minutes was to give birth to a professional teaching force.

Minimally there are three indicators of professionalism:

- A rigorous training process which endows participants with a legitimate expertise, which means they can fulfil a role more successfully than the untrained.
- A means of communication which enables a shared outlook and a sense of common purpose to emerge.
- An acceptance among those who are the supposed beneficiaries of the work, status, expertise and value of those who claim to be professional.

While the third of these measures remains problematic, the 1846 minutes guaranteed that at least an elite minority of elementary teachers were trained. What is exciting about the 1840s is witnessing the emergence of a shared consciousness among teachers. This took two forms: the creation of an educational press and the formation of teacher associations.

Asher Tropp (1957), in an early history of the teaching profession, has identified no less than 50 journals created in the 1840s and 1850s to serve the burgeoning interest in education and the needs of the newly trained teachers. While many of these journals were read only by a social elite, there were those, such as the *Educational Expositor*, which were written and read by the teaching profession. They were the nineteenth-century equivalent of blogging and twittering – a means of passing on news and shaping opinions.

One of the hallmarks of a profession is the belief that the practices engaged in by an individual, and the values which underpin them, are a shared currency among all those practising that particular trade. This involves creating formal agencies to promote systematic conversation aimed at professional enhancement. Teachers as early as the 1830s had begun to form local associations, but these were often under the supervision of the local clergy. A decade later these local associations were beginning to come together into national bodies and to assert their professional autonomy. Thus, the General Associated Body of Church Schoolmasters in England and Wales was formed, complete with what Tropp (1957) calls a 'militant wing' that wanted to exclude the clergy from membership. Some of the clergy who were very close to the policy makers were deeply unhappy at such shows of independence from those they regarded as their employees and social inferiors. John T. Smith (2009), in his study of teacher–clerical relationships in the nineteenth century, sees such clerical unhappiness with teachers as endemic to the relationship between the two professions and of such intensity that it approaches a class conflict in its proportions.

Educational Policy and Teacher Professionalism in the Mid-Nineteenth Century

The 1840s, therefore, marked the beginning of educational policy making, and one consequence of this was the beginning, too, of teachers as professionals. Undoubtedly, the scale of educational business was miniscule in comparison with today's policy juggernauts. Nevertheless, some of the preoccupations of policy makers then are still the preoccupations of today – specifically, the need to juggle the two balls of sufficient funding for education (sufficient to deliver the social ambitions held for it) and what has recently been called prudent public expenditure. By the 1850s there were those who felt that the juggler had dropped the second of these balls. It was time to retrench.

As we have argued, the fear of revolution receded in the 1850s and with it the reason for the state's investing so heavily in education. The rising cost of educational provision was a growing concern. Moreover, it was not as if the educational policy making of the 1840s had delivered unalloyed success. Government aid to voluntary educational effort was failing to deliver a universal educational system whereby every child in every town, village and hamlet in the country was guaranteed a school place. In the words of James Fraser, a man of notable influence among policy makers and a future Bishop of Manchester, there were areas 'utterly destitute' where schools had never been built by voluntary effort, consequently 'lengthening the gloom and dreariness of the surrounding waste' (Newcastle Report, 1861, p. 55). It was not just an expensive system then but also a failing one in the eyes of some.

However, the relationship between policy maker and policy is rarely exclusively a matter of shillings and pence. The heads of those responsible for deciding policy also contain images of how society is currently shaped, the part education will play in that shaping, and the extent to which the state has to actively play a part in these complex processes. Kay Shuttleworth, the first Secretary to the Committee on Education, believed that the social structure he subscribed to was in danger of collapsing and that education could help to prevent this. The state had a responsibility to actively promote education. His successor as secretary was Ralph Lingen whose head contained very different and less apocalyptic visions of the current state of society.

One of the ongoing policy debates of the 1850s was what to do with the legacy of the policy initiatives of the 1840s. One of these legacies was Kneller Hall, a training college for schoolmasters employed in workhouses. Workhouses had been created in 1834 as an instrument to provide both support and discipline for the destitute poor. They were widely hated and feared by the poor for the harshness of the regime they applied to those placed in their 'care'. Plans to train the teachers of the child inhabitants of the workhouse had never been successfully implemented, leading to a debate about how best to dispose of the Kneller Hall albatross.

The ensuing debate among the policy makers reveals their assumptions about society, education and the role of the state. For Lingen it was clear that workhouse children were the equivalent to the inhabitants of prisons and as such were 'the creatures of the state' who might legitimately lay claim to some state finance (memorandum from R[alph] L[ingen]on the future of Kneller Hall, PRO 30/29/19/2/1, dated 13 April 1853). The phrase 'creatures of the state' remains chilling more than 150 years later but is indicative of the way in which for mid-century policy makers society was fragmenting into different social strata, of which the bottommost layer – the paupers and criminals (and they were seen as virtually interchangeable) – were likely to receive state-funded education.

These, then, were the questions which exercised the thinking of policy makers by the late 1850s:

- What was a reasonable level of state financial support for education?
- Should educational provision continue to be essentially a matter of voluntary initiative?
- Would a system of local taxation provide more secure funding for education?
- Should parents be compelled to send their children to school?

As we have seen, the answers to these questions were complicated by the policy makers' assumptions about the social structure they inhabited.

In an attempt to arrive at some answers to these dilemmas, the government decided to appoint a Royal Commission to investigate elementary education. Commissions were already an established instrument available to politicians by the mid-nineteenth century, although this was their first application to elementary education. Their format too was well established. Commissioners would be appointed from among those worthies with some knowledge of the subject to be investigated, chaired by a well-connected figure who might command some support across factional politics. Assistant commissioners would act as field investigators and expert witnesses would be invited to share their expertise with the commissioners. This was broadly to be the formula for the next 150 years for a series of commissions which have investigated a range of educational topics and influenced to a greater or lesser extent educational policy.

The 1858 Commission was chaired by the Duke of Newcastle, hence the Newcastle Commission, and reported in 1861. The establishment of the commission in 1858 reveals the extent to which the theory of the Royal Commissions – the dispassionate and objective weighing up of evidence to reach unimpeachable recommendations – is at odds with the actual practice of commissions. The Commission consisted of seven men, none of whom were especially enthusiastic about Kay Shuttleworth's policy creation. The composition of the Commission had been largely engineered by Ralph Lingen as he responded to the large number of lobbyists advocating the candidacy of this or that individual. In February 1858 Lingen wrote:

> The best turn which in my opinion, the Commission could take, would be while doing justice to the results of the present system, as far as they go, to condemn the principle by exploring its essential uncertainties and complications as well as the amount of centralisation which it involves. [It] should

exclude those who are deaf to everything but the cry for larger grants more laxly administered. (Lingen to Granville, 14 February 1858. Granville Papers PRO 30/29, Box 24, Part 2)

The Commission's recommendations reflected to some extent Lingen's views, but they were not the mere mouthpiece of the Education Committee Secretary.

Their report advocated two policy initiatives in an attempt to reconcile a simplified system of adequate funding for schools with a guarantee of quality of provision. Schools would henceforth be funded out of local taxation in the form of rates charged on property and administered by 'County Boards'. This would compel local landowners, who in the view of the commissioners had been neglectful of their responsibilities, to contribute to school provision. Secondly, this rate aid would be distributed on the basis of the results of each individual child's ability to read, write and do arithmetic. Prize schemes, whereby children were rewarded with modest prizes for good attendance, were a familiar part of the 1850s educational landscape. However, the commissioners discovered that a scheme in the Diocese of Bath and Wells awarded the prizes not to the children but to their teachers. For the first time, but certainly not the last in the history of education, a local practice was extrapolated into a national policy.

In 1856, the office of Vice President of the Education Department was introduced, with the expressed intention, John Hurt (1972, p. 164) argues, of overseeing the work of the civil servants running the department. The need for political control of those charged with putting policy into effect is yet another of those themes emerging in the mid-century which were to persist to this day. At the time of the Newcastle Commission, Robert Lowe was Vice President of the Education Department and thereby the politician in charge of education. He had no interest in rate-aided education but seized on the Commission's idea of examinations to measure performance with alacrity. In 1861, a New Code was published, which abolished the 1846 grants system replacing it with single payments to schools based on children's performance in what came to be called the three Rs (reading, writing and 'rithmetic). From the age of 3 children would be examined in 'standards' and would earn their school 2 shillings and 2 old pence for each pass in each of the three subjects. The examinations were to be conducted annually by HMIs and henceforth, it seems, the maximum educational value of a child was set at 6 shillings and 6 old pence.

The response to the New Code could have been predicted. There was almost universal outrage. The clergy resented the exclusion of religion from the subjects to be tested. School managers suspected that the proposals were a thinly disguised attack on the levels of school funding. Teachers saw the policy as a threat to their livelihoods and an undermining of the advances they had made in professional status since 1846. Even HMIs were alarmed by the prospect of their new inquisitorial role. Lowe described his own Educational Office as being in revolt from 'the teaboy to Matthew Arnold' (the Chief Inspector). Poor Henry Bellairs, the HMI for the Bristol area, complained bitterly that the ruction in his area had been such as to bring on his gout.

The policy-making procedure whereby government publishes a white paper to gauge opinion had not yet been established, but the events of 1861–1862 have that feel to them.

The hostility to the New Code was such that the government was forced into concessions: attendance grants would be maintained; there would be continued financial support for teacher training; and children would not be tested before the age of 5. However, the government stood by the main provision of the Code. In 1862, in what was now the Revised Code it was declared that henceforth school income and therefore teacher pay would be partly determined by the children's examination performance. 'Payments by results' had arrived.

Voice Box 1.1

HMI John Norris to Lord Granville, 14 December 1855

Some five or six years ago several Teachers Associations have been formed in my District, and I believe in other districts. Their purpose·was mutual improvement – so long as they retained their *local* and business like character, they seemed to me in every way good and I was glad to attend their meetings as often they invited me to do so.

Of late years I have noticed a growing restlessness among them and I have traced it to an ambitious effort on the part of the metropolitan teachers to bind together and centralise these provincial associations coextensive with the country. Meetings have been held in London and periodicals started with this in view, all more or less indicative of restlessness and a desire on the part of teachers to render themselves more independent – hoping to gain by union what they might lose in Patronage . . .

The fact is they are passing through a stage, which I suppose all young men, young societies, young nations pass through – a self-conscious stage, sensitive and impatient. Now with a schoolboy that does not signify – he does something very ridiculous, gets well snubbed and grows wiser! And Lingen seems to think we may let the same self correcting process take its course with the teachers. Let things go on – present perhaps some vastly absurd memorial to Government and then give them a smashing snub.

- How would you describe Norris's attitudes to teachers?
- Why do you think he might hold these beliefs?
- What do you think will be the effect on policy if such attitudes are widely held by those responsible for educational policy?

Of course, not all of those who influenced or made policy were as hostile to teachers as Norris. James Fraser, Assistant Commissioner to the Newcastle Commission, expressed some reservations about teachers in his private correspondence: 'even certificated teachers' in his view, failed to pay sufficient attention to the 'staples'. Nevertheless, in his report he wrote of the 'conscientiousness of the great majority of this body of men and women' with 'sterling qualifications' for their work (Newcastle Report, 1861, Vol. 2, p. 86). Significantly, the Newcastle Commissioners in their final report chose to ignore evidence such as Fraser's in favour of much more hostile attitudes to teachers.

The Revised Code illustrates the dramatic relationship which can exist between educational policy and teacher status. In the years following the Code teacher salaries fell along with recruitment to the profession. The number of educational journals declined, although teachers continued to meet in their various societies partly to agitate for the ending of what they saw as the pernicious effects of the 1862 Code. Historians have tended to see the negative impact of the Code on teachers as an unfortunate by-product of the preoccupation of the policy makers with cost cutting and getting value for money. We would argue that managing teachers, ensuring that they were teaching appropriate content in appropriate ways, was central to policy making at the time. Moreover, the suspicion of teachers in the quasi-private world of their classroom, however well trained, has been an enduring theme of policy ever since.

Educational Policy and Teacher Professionalism in the Late Nineteenth Century

The Revised Code may have successfully reined in educational expenditure and teacher professional independence. However, it did little to address the central weaknesses of the mid-Victorian elementary school system: the inability of a voluntary system to ensure that schools were built where they were most needed or to guarantee that children actually went to school. Policy makers for the next 30 years after 1862 were preoccupied with trying to resolve these issues.

In the 1860s a number of unsuccessful attempts were made to introduce rate-aided education as advocated by the Newcastle Commission, but it was not until the election of a Liberal government in 1868 that such a policy became a realistic proposition. In 1870, William Forster, the Vice President of the Education Committee, introduced a parliamentary bill whereby local Boards of Education were to be established wherever there was an insufficiency of effective school provision. These boards would be empowered to levy rates to build, equip and run schools financed by local taxation. They were also empowered to pass local bylaws to compel parents to send their children to school if they so wished.

The passage of Forster's bill was delayed by disputes about the nature of the religious teaching which would take place in the new Board schools: should denominational religion be permitted or should the schools be 'unsectarian'? Eventually a compromise whereby religious teaching was permitted provided it was without 'catechism or religious formularies distinctive of any particular denomination', enabled Forster's bill to become law.

From 1870, therefore, the ambitions of the educational policy makers of the 1840s to create a national elementary school system at last began to be realized. Forster, with great political skill, had assuaged the concerns of the denominational interests of the Anglican and Roman Catholic churches in particular by guaranteeing the continued existence of the voluntary schools. At the same time, the new Board schools would ensure that there was sufficiency of school places. Reality turned out a little differently, of course, as is often the case with policy. Board schools were sometimes built in order to challenge the monopoly of church schools while in other areas rate payers could be slow to saddle themselves with additional taxation. Also the 'voluntary' schools felt acutely disadvantaged by the superior resources of the Board schools and their power to compel attendance. The latter concern was partly remedied by the Sandon Act of 1876, which empowered the denominational schools to compel children to attend schools, followed eventually by a parliamentary act in 1890 setting a national school leaving age at 13. Schooling could not simultaneously be compulsory and paid for, so in 1891 elementary education also became free.

The legislative record of the introduction of compulsory education perhaps conceals a more complex process by which educational policy gets made and in some ways unmade as it is happening. Even after 1891 it remained permissible for factory and mill owners to employ 12- and 13-year-olds provided these children also spent half their day in school. The 'half time system', as it was called, remained part of the experience of large numbers of young people growing up in the north of England well into the 1920s. Economic need, which as we shall see commanded a growing presence in educational discourse, could cut both ways. In general terms, business might agree that educational investment helped to foster skills which industry required, but in practice it was difficult to set aside the nimble fingers and cheap wages of children.

Parents too frequently tried to evade their responsibility to send their children to school. Attendance Officers (or 'Board men' as the author remembers them still being called in 1970s Staffordshire) and the prosecutions they instituted were widely resented by parents. Compulsion and the use of corporal punishment were the persistent focus of working-class antagonism to formal education. The history of the introduction of compulsory education is a chastening reminder that all educational policy has unforeseen consequences.

Voice Box 1.2

From a Speech by Mr W. E. Forster, Vice President of the Council, introducing the Elementary Education Bill in the House of Commons, 17 February 1870

Upon the speedy provision of elementary education depends our industrial prosperity. It is no use trying to give technical teaching to our artisans without elementary education; uneducated labourers – and many of our labourers are utterly uneducated – are, for the most part, unskilled labourers, and if we leave our work-folk any longer unskilled, notwithstanding their strong sinews and determined energy, they will become over matched in the competition of the world. Upon this speedy provision depends also, I fully believe, the good, the safe working of our constitutional system. To its honour, Parliament has latterly decided that England shall in future be governed by popular government. I am one of those who would not wait until the people were educated before I trusted them with political power. If we had thus waited we might have waited long for education; but now we have given them political power we must not wait any longer to give them education. There are questions demanding

⇨

answers, problems which must be solved, which ignorant constituencies are ill-fitted to solve. Upon this speedy provision of education depends also our national power. Civilized communities throughout the world are massing themselves together, each mass being measured by its force; and if we are to hold our position among men of our own race or among the nations of the world we must make up the smallness of our numbers by increasing the intellectual force of the individual (in Maclure, 1973).

- Why does Forster believe that his government needs to do more to ensure the provision of education?
- Research Forster's biography to find out more about his contribution to the development of educational policy.

Forster's speech is indicative of ways in which the mind-set of educational policy makers was shifting in the last quarter of the nineteenth century. The connection between the appropriate exercise of political power and elementary education would not have been out of place 25 years earlier, although the embrace of democracy (much more restricted than Forster implies) was new. Where the rhetoric departs from earlier scripts is in the ways in which elementary education is now connected to 'technical teaching' and both are to be harnessed to national need to compete internationally. A new hare is up and running: education now has an economic purpose in a world of global competitiveness. It is a policy hare which is still out there in the minds of today's policy makers.

According to Martin Pugh (1994) Forster's speech would have been typical of the growing concern at the time that the 1860s marked the peak of British industrial domination and the 1870s saw the beginning of the slow process of relative decline. Even in the 1860s, Pugh argues, 'British strength was her capacity to mobilise her human and physical resources for sophisticated and profitable economic activities more effectively than her rivals' (1994, p. 3), rather than population size, for example. What is less evident in Forster's speech but manifested in the debate which prolonged its parliamentary passage, is contemporary concern as to the limits to the state's educational role. As early as 1833, the radical Member of Parliament, John Roebuck had proposed State provision of elementary schools, but the proposal had foundered on hostility to such an extension of State power. For the next 40 years policy makers had shied away from policies which smacked of state control of education, albeit that the country's principal educator – the Church of England – was an established church and hugely influential in the making of policy. The minutes of 1846 may have extended the educational power of the state, but the essential attribute of a state system, building schools, remained a voluntary and thereby 'private' matter.

The reasons for resisting direct state provision of schools were varied. There were practical concerns that such provision might 'drive out' voluntary endeavour, resulting in little overall gain. Among policy makers there was also a widespread belief that British industrial power had been built on the basis of the bonfire which had been lit in the 1840s under trade tariffs and restrictive practices. It seemed illogical to introduce 'free trade' in one sphere of national policy while excluding it from another. There were also more philosophical concerns about the extent to which it was legitimate for the state to intrude into relationships between parents and their children together with an entirely prosaic self-interest in avoiding increased taxation.

The Forster Act marked a new point of settlement in the public–private debate. The act did not create a state educational system. Part of the purpose of the act was to help protect voluntary school provision, and this was enshrined in the notion of a 'dual' system whereby the new Board schools would co-exist with church schools. Even the former were conceived of as 'local', to be established and maintained by their local communities. However, the state had now decreed that the provision of school places was no longer a matter of choice; that the financing and powers of Board schools were to be legislatively enshrined; and that so far as religious teaching was concerned, there were limits in what Board school teachers could teach their children. The line between public and private had been redrawn in favour of the state.

To return now to the idea with which we began this chapter: that educational policy making can only be understood by reference to the social history of the period and that social class was the dominant feature of that social landscape. It has been argued that Chartism in particular provoked educational policy makers in the 1830s and 1840s into policy making that made overt reference to the need for schools to remedy class conflict. The 1850s was a period of relative social quiet with corresponding policy retrenchment and a make-do-and-mend approach to the outcomes of the great policy initiatives of the previous decade. By the 1870s, however, a kind of class society had emerged which called for new educational policies harnessing the people of this new world to national agendas around economic competition and imperial power. Kay Shuttleworth's rhetoric, which appeared overblown to some cooler heads even in the 1840s, would no longer serve in the 1870s and 1880s.

The growing conviction among policy makers that education had an economic role led to a developing interest in technical education and access to levels of education beyond that of the elementary school. This in turn raised questions about who exactly should benefit from state educational expenditure. Was it any longer justifiable to see such expenditure as being directed solely at working-class children? These are the emerging policy themes of the closing years of the nineteenth century, which lie more properly with the next chapter. However, what is significant is the way in which working-class voices begin to figure, albeit in a small way, in the process of policy decision making.

Summary

In the nineteenth century the class society took on a particular shape and form in response to industrialization and urbanization which included profound challenges to the English state. Governmental partial financing of elementary schools was one kind of response to this challenge. Government involvement in schools necessitated the creation of policy machinery – an Education Office, staffed by civil servants, and political officers of the state to oversee their work – which is still with us today. The principal function of this machinery was to ensure that educational financing was well spent, which in turn led to the creation and subsequent managing of the teaching profession. Teachers' professionalism, as a consequence, was both enhanced and inhibited by the exercise of policy. By the end of the century, international competition was encouraging policy makers to rethink the *raison d'être* for investing in education with the consequent effect on policy. It is this last point which marks the beginning of our exploration of policy in the twentieth century.

Useful References

Hurt, J. (1972), *Education in Evolution*. London: Paladin.

Lawson, J., and Silver, H. (1973), *A Social History of Education*. London: Methuen.

Tropp, A. (1957), *The School Teachers: The Growth of the Teaching Profession in England and Wales from 1800 to the Present Day*. London: Heinemann.

2

Policy Making 1890–1945

Secondary Education for All

Introduction

The story of educational policy making in the first half of the twentieth century is laid out against a grand backdrop of events that shaped the policy-making process. The first of these events is *war*. British history in the first half of the twentieth century is dominated by two world wars between 1914 and 1918 and war again in 1939–1945. In both cases, the principal antagonist was Germany, but both wars were worldwide in scale. In both cases, too, the wars were total in that for the first time in British experience virtually the entire adult population was recruited to support the war effort. For Marwick (1970), war is a moment of major *discontinuity* unsettling previous social and economic beliefs and practices. The effects of such discontinuities are contestable. War can bring in its wake major social transformation: equally it can create an appetite for retrenchment and an insistence on the preservation of prewar norms. What seems incontestable is that total war has the effect of empowering the state as it involves itself in the lives of its citizens in ways undreamed of in peacetime.

War was not the only dislocating force in the first half of the previous century. The period was also seared by *economic depression* in 1921–1922 and then by the Wall Street crash of 1929 and the ensuing depression which for many lasted through most of the 1930s. While much of southern England enjoyed a relatively prosperous decade in the 1930s, large parts of the old industrial areas of the north, Scotland and Wales were plunged into poverty.

The third and final theme of significance to education policy is the slow *emergence during this period of a democratic state*. For much of the nineteenth century, the British state was an aristocratic one in that any entitlement to vote was tied to property ownership. Democracy, however, is more than the entitlement to vote. Universal enfranchisement redefines the relationship between government and people as the legitimacy of the former rests on the manifest support of the latter. In order to make this happen the British political system had to ensure that political parties evolved from expressions of factional interests among a political elite to dynamic bodies which could lay some claim to representing ideologies and interests among the people as a whole. At the beginning of the century the Liberal Party managed this transition successfully, chalking up a series of election victories before surrendering its claim to represent the urban working class to the growing strength of the Labour Party. In many ways, however, the political skills of both these parties paled into insignificance when compared with that of the Conservatives and their formidable capacity to appeal to an electorate across gender and class divisions.

The Making of Policy Machinery

In order to be effective, policy makers require the means of putting policy decisions into practice. They are also likely to be more effective – to ensure their policies have greater 'stickability' – if their policy machine provides for two-way communication. This way they know how their policies are being implemented and received. We have already seen how the first educational policy machinery, consisting of an education department in Whitehall overseen by the Committee of the Privy Council and aided and abetted by a team of inspectors, was set up in the 1840s. From the 1870s, school boards began to provide local educational machinery, but they were only set up where there was believed to be a need for board schools and the political will to address this need. In truth, at the beginning of our period educational administration from the viewpoint of those in government was something of a hotchpotch.

In 1888, parliament passed the Local Government Act, which created 62 county councils and a large number of county boroughs where the population was in excess of 50,000. This meant that for the first time there was a standardized national system of local government. These new county councils quickly began to acquire new powers, including the power to improve technical education in their areas by making grants to secondary schools and to provide scholarships in technical subjects. As we shall see, these were the precursors to more far-reaching innovations in the years to come.

In 1899, central government machinery was reformed with the creation of a Board of Education to subsume the powers previously residing with the Education Department, the Science and Art Department, and the Charity Commission. In keeping with the emergence of cabinet government, the Board was to be headed by the Minister of Education. Of greater immediate significance perhaps was the appointment of Robert Morant as the board's first permanent secretary.

The election of a Conservative government in 1886 under Lord Salisbury ushered in a long period of Tory hegemony, broken only by a short period of Liberal government.

The minds of policy makers in the 1890s were exercised by two major concerns: how to respond to the evident appetite for education above and beyond that provided by the elementary schools; and how to address the growing disparity in funding between the rate-financed board schools and their voluntary counterparts dependent on Whitehall grants and largely church financing.

In March 1902, Arthur Balfour, shortly to become Prime Minister, introduced a bill into the House of Commons to replace over 2,000 school boards with 318 local educational authorities who in the future would also be responsible for secondary and technical education in their areas as well as elementary schools, including those hitherto under the control of the voluntary bodies. In return for providing the buildings, voluntary managers would continue to appoint teachers but running costs would be met from the rates. The bill provoked a political storm. The Nonconformist groups, that is, those in the Protestant churches who had broken with the Church of England during two centuries of troubled religious history, objected to religious teaching being paid for with taxpayers money. They also feared that Nonconformist children would be forced to attend church schools. The Liberal opposition took up their cause in parliament while outside there was a long campaign of passive resistance. Nevertheless in December the bill became law. With the passing of the act the country had an administrative system which was to endure for most of the twentieth century. The new local educational authorities could provide the means by which policy could be translated into practice reasonably effectively. Next, we need to probe the thinking which lay behind this change.

Secondary Education for All?

As we saw in the previous chapter, Victorian policy makers were largely preoccupied with the provision of elementary education. For them, a working-class child's education would at best be completed by the age of 10, 11, or 12. By and large, secondary education was a matter for parents to finance and took place for the upper classes in the great public schools, while those of more modest means sent their children to many hundreds of private 'academies' which sprang up in the period. The exception was the 40 or so endowed grammar schools which existed in the 1860s. These had been founded by land or money bequeathed by earlier generations for the education of 'poor scholars' who were largely boys. As charities, these schools came under the auspices of the Charity Commission. In 1865, the Taunton Commission investigated endowed schools and as a consequence, the Endowed Schools Act followed, which increased the number of scholarships available to send children to these schools. That apart, policy makers largely ignored secondary education before the 1880s.

In 1890, the central educational preoccupation of government was still elementary schools, especially the funding of the voluntary schools. There was also a growing debate about the age to which children should be compelled to go to school. In 1890, this was set at 13, but children could be exempted at 10 if they reached a required standard. This was quickly raised to 11 and then 12 but there it remained until 1918. Lawson and Silver (1973) suggest that in 1914, 40 per cent of children were still leaving school before the age of 12. Of course, to argue that government policy makers were not overly concerned with secondary education before 1890 is not to say that secondary education was not happening. At a local level, there was growing provision of secondary education for working-class children, albeit a small minority. A number of school boards in the large cities took advantage of the relaxation of the Revised Code to establish higher elementary schools. In 1889, the Technical Instruction Act enabled the Science and Art Department to promote science teaching in such schools by providing some funding. It seems that by the 1890s, the growing awareness of Britain's industrial decline relative to Germany and the United States, the technological nature of what has been termed the 'second industrial revolution', and the hugely increasing demand for clerical and retail workers created an appetite for education beyond the three Rs.

Those responsible for determining government educational policy clearly noted these developments and did what they had done for most of the century – appointed a Royal Commission to investigate secondary education. The Bryce Commission, named after its chairman, James Bryce, reported in 1895. It concluded that the majority of endowed schools had improved in the past 25 years. It noted too that provision for middle-class girls had increased. It suggested that the grammar school curriculum was being modernized and the members of the Commission were keen to preserve a place for Latin teaching. On the whole, the schools remained overwhelmingly middle class while providing some limited access to the children of poor parents via scholarships. The Commission's recommendations were mostly to do with creating an effective administrative system for secondary education: a central authority for secondary education under the control of a Minister of Education; an Educational Council to advise the minister and act as a body to register teachers; and local authorities for secondary education drawn from county councils with the power to build and maintain schools (Maclure, 1973).

There is a clear umbilical cord between the Bryce Commission and the 1902 Education Act. The temptation, however, is to extrapolate from the sweet reason of James Bryce and his fellow commissioners and to see the act as an administrative necessity to simplify an overcomplicated educational system (e.g. see Eaglesham, 1967). The correspondence of politicians, civil servants and others close to the machinery of government tell a more complex story. As has already been argued, policy cannot be understood without some insight into the mental maps – the ways of understanding – of those driving policy. This was more complicated to achieve in 1900 than it had been in 1850 when policy makers, policy implementers, and policy influencers often shared the same almost familial world of university college, Whitehall office, London salon and country estate.

By 1900, in contrast, political parties had emerged as something more than essentially different factions of the same landed and industrial elite. Both the Liberals and the Conservatives were seeking in different ways to validate their claims to represent an urbanized population.

The Labour Party with its claim to be the authentic voice of the working class was not created until 1906 but its nascent forms were established in the 1890s. Trades unions were established among some groups of workers and they were counterbalanced by employer organizations. The school boards and the new county councils were developing cadres of informed educational opinion while elementary school teachers successfully organized their first national union. Nor had the traditional providers of the nation's schools disappeared: the Church of England, the Roman Catholic Church, and the Nonconformists (the latter largely in opposition to the first two) retained a formidable, possibly premier, presence in educational politics. Policy makers at the turn of the century were surrounded by a veritable cacophony of voices telling them where to direct policy.

Nevertheless, within the 'din' it is possible to detect some core beliefs about secondary education. The nineteenth-century secondary system, such as it was, was emphatically a stratified system. There were schools for the upper classes, schools for the middle classes, and a very few schools for a tiny number of very able working-class children. The concept of social mobility – that individuals could move out of the occupation, social class or both into which they were born and education was the means of so doing – was not widely subscribed to by policy makers or anybody else very much. By and large you did what your parents had done except where industrial change intervened. (My great great grandfather was an agricultural worker but my great grandfather was a railway worker. My grandfather was a railway worker while my father began work as a railway worker albeit as a clerk because educational opportunity had intervened.)

What, then, was the purpose of secondary education if not to foster social mobility, and how was what we would see as the manifest inequalities of the stratified system understood? William Rogers, a London clergyman and a great founder of schools, provides one kind of answer. Ruminating at a school-prize-giving event on the criticism that some of the schools he built were 'exclusive', that is, excluded working-class children, he declared:

> People rode first class, second class and third class but they all arrived at the same place. So it was with schools. Some might go to one class of schools, some to another, but the object of each case was the same – to make children good citizens.

He did not expand in this particular speech on what this railway terminus – the 'good citizen' – looked like but he did suggest what the middle-class coach should not provide:

> This evening he was addressing for the most part those who were riding so to speak in the second class carriages. In these schools they gave the children a good and useful education without attempting to make the girls fine ladies or the boys swaggering fellows about town. (Address by Rogers, 26 December 1874. *City Press* newspaper cuttings held by the Bishopsgate Institute)

The notion of good citizenship subscribed to by the likes of Rogers, who was one of the earliest creators of scholarships, was porous and friable in that it allowed educational ambition and notions of individual social mobility to seed themselves. Thus, reviewing the educational ideologies which had circled around his life's work toward the end of his life, Rogers considered what was educationally appropriate for a child who was now staying in school until age 13:

> You may keep it still at the 3Rs and the effect will be that it will become dulled and wearied. Or you may open to its enquiring intellect the first gates of higher knowledge, and by varied and deeper instruction afford it certainly less present monotony and perhaps some future happiness. Is there a doubt which is the better course? And I commend this view to many worthy people who talk very thoughtlessly about the over education of the poor. (Hadden, 1888, p. 202)

Not unnaturally, Rogers took pride in the fact that some of the boys [*sic*] who had attended the middle-class schools he helped to create had gone onto careers in the universities, especially in science, and the civil service, and many thousands went into the banks and counting houses of the city (ibid., pp. 170–1).

William Rogers is a good example of what today we would call a nongovernment organization promoting educational causes. As a Church of England clergyman, he was never a politician (in the formal sense) or a civil servant although he did serve on the Newcastle Commission. However, as a man of energy and creativity with a formidable network of contacts in the Church, the City of London, and the Liberal Party (he was a friend of the Prime Minister, Lord Rosebery), he was more than a promoter of state educational policies. His work formulated and promoted policy from outside of government always pointing in the direction of educational expansion. His views on 'middle-class' education, citizenship, the acceptance if not outright promotion of social mobility, and the ways in which these slid into a curriculum which begins to look like a secondary education provide a door through which we can enter the mind-set of policy makers at the turn of the century.

The danger with history is reading it backward. In this instance, because we know that 50 years into the twentieth century universal provision of secondary education was realized, then policy makers in 1900 become heroes or villains according to how they are positioned vis-à-vis that trajectory. What had undoubtedly happened in the last quarter of the nineteenth century was a welling up from outside central government of a demand for an expanded education for more children. For how many, in what form, and to what ends was what policy makers were wrestling with.

The terms of their debates about secondary education were complicated. Some expressed attitudes which seemed to belong firmly in the past, while others were struggling to give voice to ideas which would become part of a twentieth-century narrative about education. This can be seen in the correspondence of Frederick Temple, the Archbishop of Canterbury, and as such the recipient of the concerns of his Church members and an assiduous communicator with a largely sympathetic Tory government. He was in short at the heart of the turn-of-the-century policy nexus. In a typical piece of correspondence, a Mr Vaughan Davies, commenting on a recent Temple speech, wrote:

> You remarked that the present extent of education was rather too wide and that a large portion of the present teaching was of no real use whatever. I am quite of your opinion and am tempted to

ask whether you do not consider that at present we are educating the industrial classes beyond their position and that it may become a National Danger.

At present the Government are devising all manner of schemes to induce lads to enter the mercantile navy, as a reserve for the Royal Navy and agriculturalists are complaining of the want of labourers. Before education was made compulsory and free, boys were willing to take employment as Sailors and Farmhands but now we are educating them to the extent that they quite look down upon manual labour and rush to the towns and flood the offices and kindred employment that the Middle Classes are completely glutted while the industrial classes are educated out of the latter.

On which Temple had scribbled:

I did not say that the Education now given to children of the Industrial Classes was beyond their position but beyond their capacities. (Temple, 1899)

The letter and, even more, Temple's correction reveal some of the terms of the secondary education debate. They include:

- There were still those who were fearful about overeducating large numbers of working-class children.
- Secondary education was widely assumed to be predominantly a matter for boys.
- The notion was, as expressed by Temple, that 'capacity' – or intelligence set the ceiling on educational opportunities.

None of these attitudes disappeared entirely in the coming century. Fears about education certainly surfaced whenever the possibility of expanding university education was raised, although social class became an implicit rather than explicit feature of the discourse. Girls were going to have to wait a long time to obtain equal educational opportunities with boys. It was Temple's articulation of 'capacity', however, which would be the dominant feature of secondary education in the twentieth century. It was assumed that, by and large, all children up to the age of 11 would benefit from a broadly shared curriculum, and while 'intelligence' might determine their successful acquisition of knowledge, it should not produce stratified schools. Secondary education for reasons to do with 'capacity' was conceptualized differently as inevitably a selective process.

The 1902 Education Act was very much shaped by the social thinking of the policy makers and those like Temple who sought to influence them. In 1899, a test case was brought against the London School Board by which the board was surcharged by the official auditor, J. B. Cockerton, for providing a form of secondary education. As a consequence, such provision became illegal, paving the way for the 1902 Act. In spite of their political differences, the authors of the Act, who Lawson and Silver (1973) argue were the two conservative politicians John Gorst and Arthur Balfour, the Fabian and London County councillor Sydney Webb and the civil servant Robert Morant shared many social assumptions. Like William Rogers, Gorst was fond of the railway metaphor and convinced that people travelling in different 'classes' was simply how the world was. The effect was to try to ideologically, and in policy terms too, marginalize those who considered that such assumptions were a grave injustice to working-class children, forever riding in the third class railway carriage. While Morant, Balfour and certainly Webb were much less sanguine about social stratification and more enthusiastic about expanding secondary educational provision, they, like Temple, would have been unconvinced about the notion of universal secondary education.

This can be seen clearly in the way in which the Regulations for Secondary Education were drawn up by Robert Morant, then Secretary to the Board of Education, in 1904. These were not anti-science but they were antivocational education of the kind offered by some of the school boards prior to 1902. By in effect defining a core secondary curriculum as English, languages including Latin, and maths and science, they ensured that children's ability, or 'capacity', would be measured in terms of a traditional, subject-based curriculum. This was to have a profound effect on future educational policy making and generations of children's experience of secondary schooling.

Secondary educational opportunity did expand over the next few years. Five hundred grant-aided schools in 1904 had grown to a thousand by 1914. The number of children attending these schools trebled from 64,000 to 188,000. Even technical education managed to retain a foothold in the continued provision of some higher elementary schools, albeit of uncertain status. In 1917 the examination system was reformed. Subjects were grouped in three areas: English, languages and maths and science – and access to grammar school was on the basis of five passes to include one from each curriculum area. In spite of this, secondary education remained a minority experience. Only 5 per cent of children attended secondary schools. For most, elementary education was what they got until they left school at age 14 or earlier.

Secondary Education for All: The Impact of the Labour Movement and War

We have argued that the educational policy makers before 1914 were indifferent to the possibility of universal secondary education, which, in any case, they defined in a narrow way. Those who thought differently lacked the political power to influence policy. This was to change in the second quarter of the twentieth century under the twin impact of war and the influence of the Labour movement.

Prior to the outbreak of war in 1914, attitudes to social policy making were shifting. The long period of Conservative power was broken in the general election of 1906 when the Liberal Party was elected with an 84-seat majority in the House of Commons. Additionally, for the first time, parliament now included 53 Labour members of whom 29 were sponsored by the newly formed Labour representation committee. The new Liberal government was not exactly in the business of social transformation but it was aware that the massive economic growth of the previous century, while bringing wealth to some, had exacerbated the poverty of those living in the city slums and the less-evident poverty of the countryside. The new government, however, displayed a greater appetite for state intervention to address poverty than its predecessors.

What, then, was the impact of war on this political mind-set and the policies it generated? The loss of life in the First World War was immense: 745,000 young British men were killed – 9 per cent of all those under 45 – and over 1.2 million wounded. The effects of death and pain on such a scale are impossible to measure, but Marwick (1970) argues that society in the twenties and thirties 'exhibited all the signs of having suffered a deep mental wound' (ibid., p. 63). In comparison with the Second World War, civilian casualties at around 1,500 from aircraft and warship raids were modest, but in all other respects there were daily reminders that war was now 'total': shortage of foodstuffs, rising taxation, and from 1916, the conscription of husbands, sons and brothers.

All of this fed an appetite for social change. A Ministry of Reconstruction was set up in 1917. Many reports were written on aspects of social and economic life and 'a land fit for heroes' became the slogan under which the wartime coalition government fought the 1918 election campaign. It is perhaps remarkable, therefore, how little postwar society actually changed. The Civil Service increased in size and the upper grades were open to women for the first time, always providing they did not marry. Government became more 'primeministerial', partly because of the huge personality of the incumbent, Lloyd George, who also had a taste for what was later known as 'kitchen cabinet' politics – consultation with a close group of advisers to the exclusion and chagrin of ministers. New ministries for health, transport (shorn of its powers to nationalize the railways), labour and pensions survived into the 1920s, but many of the wartime agencies were simply dismantled. Indeed, Mowat (1968) argues that this was true throughout the interwar years. Citing an earlier historian, he argues that those who knew England in 1914 would find in 1939:

> The same names on the front of chain stores, the same newspapers owned by the same press lords, the same popular brands of cigarettes and chocolate, the same popular novelists, the same football teams, and the same express trains (sometimes a little slower, sometimes a little faster by 1939). Even half the members of parliament sitting in 1939 were the same men who had sat in parliament in 1914. (ibid., p. 9)

While total war might produce an appetite for social change, it seems that the meal itself was modest. The same modesty pertained to education policy. In 1907, the government expanded the number of scholarships such that by 1914, 25 per cent of children were not paying fees for their secondary education. Of course, by the same token, 75 per cent were fee-payers, meaning that the main beneficiary of the expansion of secondary provision was the middle class. The war clearly had a detrimental effect on formal education. Demand for child labour was such that over 600,000 children were allowed at the age of 12 to work for up to 33 hours in factories while attending school for the remainder of their time.

A 'land fit for heroes' also embraced the heroes' children. In 1917, H. A. L. Fisher, President of the Board of Education, drew up an educational bill to put before parliament. For Fisher the bill was linked to the war in two ways: it was important that education provided for the physical well-being of children and youth: and secondly, educational provision should acknowledge the shared citizenry so tragically evidenced in the mud of Flanders. He criticized the 1902 Education Act for failing to provide a national system of secondary schools, but his social and educational attitudes were those of his predecessors. While recognizing that 'industrial workers' were demanding a secondary education, he tried to define and categorize this demand:

> They [industrial workers] do not want education only in order that they become better technical workmen and earn higher wages. They do not want it in order that they may rise out of their own class, always a vulgar ambition, they want it because they know that in the treasures of the mind they can find an aid to good citizenship, a source of pure enjoyment and a refuge from the necessary hardships of a life spent in the midst of clanging machinery in our hideous cities of toil. (Maclure, 1973, p. 74)

Given such a mind-set, small wonder the 1918 Act was such a mouse. The Board of Education was empowered to compel local authorities to offer a 'comprehensive' system of education, by which was meant provision from nursery through to an adequate number of senior or central school places. There was some talk of raising the school leaving age to 15 but in the end it was kept at 14. The half-time system which allowed children younger than 14 to be employed was abolished, although this was slow to be implemented and there were still 'half-timers' in some of the northern textile towns in the 1920s. By and large, though, after 1918 all children attended elementary, higher elementary or secondary schools until they were 14. The rest of the act fell victim to postwar public expenditure retrenchment – 'the Geddes axe'. Nursery provision was abandoned, teacher salaries cut and there was talk, never enacted, of beginning formal schooling at the age of 6. Not for the first time and certainly not the last, educational policy fell foul of Treasury requirements. Lawson and Silver have argued that after 1902, education:

> became an element of a new pattern of social policy at a time when Britain's world economic dominance had begun to decline, an age of both increasing international competition, not only between nations but between empires, and of world war. (1973, p. 364)

This is an overstatement. Governments did not have a social policy of which education was a part before 1920. The philosophical inability to see intellectual merit in vocational education and the conviction that 'capacity' had only been sparingly distributed among the population always set the ceiling low on a universal education. Add to this the exigencies of economics and it is small wonder that policy ambitions and outcomes were modest.

Politics was changing, though. Savage and Miles (1994, p. 80) argue that the Labour Party, which began as a defensive movement to help protect trade unions before the war, had evolved by 1920 into a party representing large sections of urban Britain. During the next 20 years it increasingly favoured state intervention into social policy, gradually abandoning earlier alternative strategies to achieve socialism. They further argue that this commitment to state intervention, particularly in education, was especially strong where women influenced local parties.

As we have seen, the concept of secondary education for all did not really exist at the beginning of the century. Even those in the emerging Labour movement thought more in terms of expanded provision to meet the needs of talented working-class children. Toward the end of the war this began to change as it occurred to some on the Left that if untalented middle- and upper-class children could obtain secondary education as a right, the same could not be denied to working-class children. In 1918, the Labour Party advocated a system of education 'which shall get rid of all class distinctions and privileges and bring to every boy and girl all the training, physical, mental and moral, literary, technical and artistic of which he is capable" (cited in Branson, 1975, p. 122). In 1922, the Labour intellectual R. H. Tawney published *Secondary Education for All* in which he attacked the organization of secondary education along class lines. For Tawney, the so-called educational ladder supposedly affording bright working-class children social mobility did no such thing. Instead, it was a greasy pole. What was needed was free secondary education for all, initially to the age of 15 and thereafter to age 16.

The Hadow Committee

In 1924, the first Labour government was elected with a commitment to prioritizing secondary education. The government lasted less than a year but it left two legacies. First, free secondary places were expanded so that by 1931, nearly half of secondary children were paying no fees at all. Second, it appointed the Hadow Committee to advise on the form of secondary education. The committee reported in 1926 and introduced new language into educational policy making. It advocated a two-stage model of education: all children would attend primary school until the age of 11 or 12 when they would all transfer to secondary school. Secondary schools would be of two kinds: the existing grammar schools would be retained for the academically able; and new schools, called modern schools, would be built with much the same curriculum but with a practical bias. The school leaving age was to be raised to 15 by 1932. The committee also went beyond a focus on systems to address the curriculum, enthusing over modern foreign languages, outlining a desirable science course and roundly condemning much current maths pedagogy.

The committee's recommendations were not implemented. The Tory government of the time was preoccupied with economic and industrial policy given the General Strike of that year, and an attempt to raise the school leaving age to 15 in 1930 was thrown out by the House of Lords. Branson attributes this in part to the conviction among the middle class that secondary education was a luxury they should not be funding except for their own children. For one Tory Member of Parliament:

> There were plenty of children who cannot learn from teachers at all. . . . They can learn only from life. Now our system of education is built upon the basis of reading, writing and arithmetic and abstractions of that sort. (in Branson, 1975, p. 127)

The Hadow Committee would not have shared this view but they did believe in different intelligences requiring different schools. This was a belief which would harden over the next 20 years and shape the eventual form of universal secondary education.

The Spens Committee

Policy makers had one more go at secondary education for all in the interwar years. In 1938 a consultative committee was set up by the board under the chairmanship of Will Spens, a university academic, to report on secondary education. The Spens Committee placed their emphasis on technical education, arguing that its relatively low status was attributable to the grammar schools' attachment to a traditional curriculum. However, instead of critically engaging with this curriculum, the committee proposed establishing technical schools oriented toward commerce and industry. The same 11-plus test, taken in order to gain admission to a grammar school could be used to select children for technical high schools. The children with aptitude for neither academic nor technical education would attend modern schools. The committee emphatically, albeit reluctantly, rejected 'multilateral' schools. This was a policy beginning to be favoured by some in the Labour movement to build secondary schools which would house all children under one roof and thereby avoid the risks of sheep and goats types of division.

The outbreak of war in 1939 reconfigured politics, policy making, and policy outcomes, not that this happened immediately. Marwick (1970, pp. 263–5) provides an inventory of the disruption and destruction caused by the war: the considerable population migration as people sought to escape from the bombing; two out of every five households affected by bomb damage; the eventual stationing of one and a half million foreign troops on British soil; the destruction of one-fifth of British schools and the evacuation of whole populations of children to the countryside. Perhaps more telling, he suggests, than these physical and psychological costs was the ideological shift in beliefs about state power, but his position on this is ambivalent:

> The most striking readjustment in the face of the challenge of war came in the separate but clearly interrelated areas of the extent and nature of government power and economic ideology informing the use of that power. On the short term what was most obvious was the colossal power again assumed by the state; on the longer term, though the state would never again give up all that it had taken unto itself, the structure of British politics still remained remarkably unchanged. (ibid., p. 270)

Beveridge and the Welfare State

Politically the main beneficiary of the war was the Labour Party with what Marwick describes as a double dividend (1970, p. 290). Churchill's coalition government included Labour ministers, but at the same time the Party and the trade unions maintained platforms from which to criticize government policy. One such example was the call by the Trade Union Council in 1940 for a complete overhaul of social services. The government responded in May 1941 by announcing that Arthur Greenwood, the Minister for Reconstruction, would carry out a comprehensive review of social service provision. The survey, Marwick argues, became the Beveridge Report and eventually the blueprint for the Welfare State as constructed after 1945.

The Beveridge Report was published in December 1942. It was largely concerned with three areas: social insurance for periods of unemployment, arguing that this should not be time limited; the provision of old age pensions; and a system of national assistance for those who fell through the insurance net. However, it was the language and ambition of the report which transcended technicalities and caught the political and popular imagination. While Beveridge suggested he was largely concerned with 'Want'; successful reconstruction could only happen, he argued, if the other great needs were addressed: ill health, inadequate education, bad housing and unemployment. In order to address these needs his report proposed a national health service, family allowances, an improved educational system, the avoidance of mass unemployment through government economic intervention and a national housing and town planning programme (Marwick, 1970, p. 309).

Butler

As early as 1941, the Board of Education had published a 'green book' setting out the intention to implement secondary education for all. This was followed in 1943 by a White Paper, 'Educational Reconstruction'. The paper is an interesting example of the entwining of policy, politics and social ideology in a wartime context. The least contentious aspect of the paper is the embrace of the Hadow principle that education should be organized in three stages: primary, secondary and further. This had become the received wisdom, and war meant that those previously opposed to the expansion of secondary education, notably employers' organizations, were now supportive. Second, the White Paper was eager to defend diversity of provision. This was a defence of the continuation of church schools (the churches remained a formidable influence on policy), and a rejection of multilateral schools as espoused by some within the Labour movement. Finally the Paper set out its egalitarian principles; within the diversity of provision there was to be parity of esteem and resource provision of different schools. Post-1945, the contradictions between these principles became more evident. Diverse schools, serving different populations, attracted different concerns in the minds of policy makers and policy implementers, including teachers and parents. In terms of our earlier metaphor, the children still tended to arrive at a different railway terminus in accordance with the school they had travelled in. In 1943 this lay in the future.

Butler produced his bill in December 1943 and it became law in 1944. All local authorities were now required to organize educational provision in accordance with the three-stages model. Secondary education was to be organized in a way which enabled the needs of different ages, abilities and aptitudes to be met. In other words, multilateral schools were rejected in favour of a tripartite system of grammar, technical and modern schools. The school leaving age was to be raised to 15 (enacted in 1947) with a view to eventually raising it to 16. Adequate specialist provision was to be made for children with special educational needs, and free milk and medical inspections were to be provided. Two parts of the act were never enacted: the provision of nursery education (again!) and compulsory part-time education in county colleges for young people to the age of 18. The position of Church schools was modified to enable them to choose between 'aided' or 'controlled' status, which traded different levels of financial support in return for different levels of local authority control. Denominational teaching could continue and all schools were now required to begin their day with an act of worship. Apart from the need to be formally registered, public schools were left untouched by the act.

Germany surrendered to the allied forces on 7 May 1945, although the war with Japan continued. Churchill offered Clement Atlee, leader of the Labour Party, the choice of continuing with the coalition government or an election. Atlee chose the latter. Both parties promised reconstruction and the full implementation of the Butler Act in their manifestos. The Conservative campaign, however, was, according to Addison (1994, p. 263), a negative one, trying to scare the electorate away from voting Labour. They failed. Labour won a landslide victory with 393 seats to the Conservative's 213. The new Prime Minister, Atlee, true to his party's election promise, implemented the 1944 Act in spite of the criticisms of some on the Left of the tripartite secondary education system. The postwar baby boomers were to be the first generation to enjoy or suffer universal secondary education provision.

Summary

Educational policy making in the first half of the twentieth century took place against a grand backdrop: War fed an appetite for change; troubled economic times reinforced the need to ensure that the nation's principal resource – the skills of its people – were able to meet the demands of the emerging global economy; and above all perhaps, the need for those with political power to claim that they governed in the interests of all the people. The period saw the development of the 'machinery' needed to implement policy – a government department, committees, and eventually local education authorities. It also saw the development of secondary education for all – with ambitions of making people into good citizens and later of fostering social mobility. The policies put in place during this period also established the pattern or the provision of schooling that we see today – essentially diverse and hierarchical and arguably divisive.

Useful References

Marwick, A. (1970), *Britain in a Century of Total War: War, Peace and Social Change 1900–1967*. Harmondsworth: Penguin Books.

Pugh, M. (1994), *State and Society: British Political and Social History: 1870–1992*. London: Edward Arnold.

Part II
Contemporary Perspectives

Policy in Practice

Introduction

After the Second World War, in a period that was characterized by both global and economic uncertainty, the education system played a crucial role in the UK's 'political, moral and economic recovery' (Porter, 2009, p. 289). During this period, education was based on principles of democracy and independence and the system was free from central government control. The Butskellite Settlement, an agreement to political consensus regarding the production of social policy, enabled education to remain free from political ideology, and any reform of the system was, therefore, the result of negotiation and compromise (Trowler, 2003, p. 35).

This state of affairs remained until the 1970s, when an oil crisis again 'fuelled' economic recession. According to Mulderrig, this resulted in the 'state being less able to legitimise capitalism through . . . the provision of adequate welfare services' (2002, p. 2). The growing cost of the education system brought it under political scrutiny and resulted in 'a shift in schools policy rhetoric towards greater economic responsiveness' (ibid.). According to Porter, 'the world had changed and the education service had to change with it' (2009, p. 292). The resulting 'more rationalistic, co-ordinated, goal-orientated approach to policy making' adopted by successive governments also heralded a more radical approach and vision for education (Trowler, 2003, p. 35).

The old 'national service, locally administered and delivered by autonomous heads and teachers' (Porter, 2009, p. 290), was, therefore, replaced by an education system 'dominated by national politicians, civil servants and quasi-civil servants, operating through centralised bureaucracies' (Fisher, 2008, p. 255). This 'paradigm shift' in education policy making, as Fisher calls it, was epitomized by the Conservative Government's Education Reform Act of 1988. The Act resulted in a highly centralized education system with a National Curriculum; testing; inspection regimes and school league tables which formed the basis of a quasi-market in education and competition between schools.

Gradually, therefore, since 1944 the government had gone from being a mere 'overseer' of the education system to a position from which it exerts overwhelming control. However, it is the last two decades, in particular, that have been characterized by the 'unprecedented political centralisation of education' (Fisher, 2008, p. 255) with education being placed at 'the vanguard of social and political change' (Mulderrig, 2002, p. 1).

When New Labour came into power in 1997 with its mantra of 'Education, Education, Education,' it espoused a vision of 'England as the major player in the new digital universe' (Porter, 2009, p. 291). In order to achieve this vision, services, including education, had to be modernized to meet the demands of globalization. Education became firmly aligned with the country's economic prosperity and economic goals dominated educational policy making. Contrary to expectations, therefore, New Labour did not abandon the marketization agenda of the previous Conservative government, but embraced it in a pragmatic fashion, perceiving education as the most effective way of getting the best out of the system (Ward, 2008). However, it did so with a vengeance, which has, according to Porter, meant that

> An unrelenting stream of orders, requirements, funding mechanisms, evaluations, target setting and privatisation has continued to be unleashed on all institutions of learning. All underline the activities of a centralised and increasingly corporate state, focussing on the production of workers for the global knowledge economy. (2009, p. 293)

As we have seen, over time societies change; their needs and wants change as do their morals and values. Educational (and other social) policies, therefore, often lose their relevance and new policy directions become an imperative. Trowler points to five key issues that emerged from the social and economic climate of the time and which New Labour's education policies had to address. These included:

- improving the standard of provision
- tackling the impacts of social disadvantage and addressing inequality in education
- improving the teaching profession
- improving the management of education
- shaping the 'Learning Society'. (2003, p. 152)

Before we go on to consider how these issues have been addressed by New Labour, it is perhaps pertinent to explain how contemporary education policy is formulated.

The Contemporary Policy-Making Process

Education policy refers to the raft of laws and initiatives that determine the shape and functioning of educational systems at both a national and a local level. An educational policy can, according to Trowler, be defined as: 'a specification of principles and actions related to educational issues, which are followed or which should be followed and which are designed to bring about desired goal' (2003, p. 95). According to Baldock *et al.* (2009, p. 5), a policy is 'an attempt to think coherently about objectives and the means to achieve them ... [and is something] ... that will occur at every organisational level'. A policy can, therefore, provide a statement of:

- the intent to make something happen
- the actions to be taken
- the organizational or administrational practice to be put in place. (ibid., p. 2)

From the government's perspective, policy making is simply considered to be 'the process by which governments translate their political vision into programmes and actions to deliver "outcomes" – desired changes in the real world' ('Modernising Government' White Paper, 1999).

Rational Policy Making

It is widely believed that policy making is carried out in a 'rational fashion' and that there is a simple, linear development from the identification of an issue or problem to the implementation of policies or practices that are designed to ameliorate it (Sutton, 1999; Trowler, 2003). In the *Rational Model* (see Figure 3.1), policy making occurs in a series of steps that include:

- recognizing the issues and defining its nature
- identifying alternative solutions and ways of dealing with the issue
- weighing up the alternatives and selecting the 'best way' forward
- implementing the policy
- evaluating the impact of the policy once it has been put into practice. (Sutton, 1999, p. 9; Trowler, 2003, p. 35. See also pages 3 & 4)

Figure 3.1 The Rational Model of Policy Making

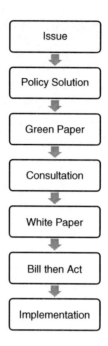

Figure 3.2 From Issue to Implementation

However, policy making is often a messy process, and this rational ideal is often far from the reality. Policy making can sometimes be simply *incremental,* that is, small changes are made to existing policies. Often, too, as Trowler suggests, policy makers just 'muddle through' responding to situations as they arise. As a consequence, policy making can appear uncoordinated and even contradictory (2003, p. 35).

In order to introduce a new policy initiative the government must first produce a *Green Paper* outlining its intentions, which is sent out for consultation to relevant stakeholders such as local authorities and schools. Following consultation and amendment, the Green Paper becomes a *White Paper* (see Figure 3.2). Some policies do not need to pass through parliament to be implemented; others, however, have to be considered by parliament in the form of a bill, where the policy undergoes further scrutiny, debate and amendment. If the proposals are accepted by both Houses of Parliament, then with the granting of Royal Assent, it becomes law, an *Act of Parliament.* Once the policy becomes entrenched in law, guidelines are sent out to local authorities, schools and other agencies that fall within its remit, which detail how the new legislation is to be implemented and how current structures and practices will be affected (see Baldock *et al.,* 2009, pp. 68–71).

Policy Borrowing

Politicians often use international comparisons, for example of attainment in assessment, to justify educational reform. Similarly, for political purposes, politicians will often use the fact that a particular policy initiative has been successfully implemented in one country as a rationale for change in their own, assuming that the policy will simply transfer from one country's context to another (see Bates and Lewis, 2009).

> . . . the workings of the global economy and the increasing interconnectedness of societies pose common problems for educational systems around the world . . . there are common problems – and what would appear to be increasingly similar education agendas. (Arnove, 2007, p. 1)

As a consequence, many policy initiatives are simply copies, adaptations or reworkings of policies or initiatives that have been developed in other countries, a process that is termed 'policy borrowing' or 'policy transfer'. As we shall see in Chapter 5, many of New Labour's child-care policies have been borrowed from America – the 'American Way'. However, policy borrowing is not always a one-way process and many initiatives developed by the UK government influence or are copied or borrowed by other national governments (see Furlong, 2002).

Policy Implementation

According to Le Métais (1997), 'education is a long term project' and any educational system is 'at any given point in time, a combination of the past, the present and the future' (1997, p. 4). With education, however, it is impossible to start afresh with a new structure; old structures and ways of working persist, and therefore, new policy directions and initiatives have to bear cognizance of such factors in order to be successful. Once implemented, policies are, therefore, considered to have a 'career' in which they are changed and adapted as they pass through the various stages of implementation at regional (local authorities) and local levels (headteachers and classroom teachers). This is because at each stage the policy is received by various stakeholders and actors, who each bring their own values, beliefs, attitudes and behaviours into the equation. Sometimes, particularly when policies are 'imposed from above', they can be met with considerable resistance, ignored or subverted. More often, however, in order to make things happen, policies are simply adapted to suit local preferences and needs (Trowler, 2003).

Policies are not static things, they ' shift and change their meanings . . . [and] are represented differently by different actors and interests' (Ball, 1994c, pp. 16–17, cited in Trowler, 2003, p. 131). The people who actually implement policy are, therefore, 'crucial actors whose actions determine the success or failure of policy initiatives' (Juma and Clarke, 1985, cited in Sutton, 1999, p. 22). Schools and teachers, therefore, are 'not mere cogs in an automatic transfer of policy-making to outcomes in practice' (Sutton, 1999, p. 22) and as a result, the outcomes of policies are rarely the same in different contexts and the impacts of policies are not always those intended by the policy maker. In order, therefore, for policies to be successfully implemented, the people who actually implement them have to have a significant ownership of how the policy is developed and put into place.

Influences on Policy Makers

Social and economic imperatives, such as child poverty, high levels of youth unemployment and economic crises often provide the drivers for new educational reforms. Increasingly, in the context of globalization and national comparisons of educational performance, governments are also keenly aware of what is happening in other countries and are influenced by the kinds of approaches that are being taken by other national governments. More important, however, all policy initiatives are to some extent inevitably determined or delimited by financial considerations and constraints. The actual measures taken by governments – the policies and initiatives they implement – are also influenced and shaped by the views of the stakeholders, particularly those who are powerful and influential; by ideological imperatives; by contemporary social constructs and discourses relating to the policy area; and by the findings of academic research.

Influential Stakeholders

Policy making is not a static process but is often the result of a dynamic interplay between the politics and personalities of those involved in the process. Thus 'policy making often is considered a privilege and is jealously guarded by those in authority' (Kumar and Sunderi, 2000, cited in Butters, n.d., p. 1). According to Neal and McLaughlin (2009), policy making involves a range of different actors, stakeholders and interest groups who function as a kind of 'policy community' in influencing or attempting to influence the direction that policy making takes (see Figure 3.3). A 'policy community' can, therefore, include government ministers, members of relevant government departments, government advisors, members of external pressure or interest groups or other organizations and individuals who might be affected by the policy. When considering the influences on the Conservative government's policy making from 1979 to 1997, Callaghan (2006) identified three key influential groups, which he termed:

- *The Politicos.* Individuals holding political office, for example, the Prime Minister, the Secretary of State, and the ministers.
- *The Regulars.* Professionals who work in the policy field including ministry officials; members of 'quangos' (quasi-autonomous nongovernmental or governmental organizations), for example, the National College for School Leadership (NCSL) and the Training and Development Agency (TDA); and representatives of government agencies (e.g. Ofsted).
- *The Irregulars.* Members of 'pressure groups', for example, the Campaign for State Education; 'think tanks', for example, the Fabian Society (Labour) and the Policy Exchange (Conservative); and government advisers.

It would be sensible to assume that because teachers are the people who most often have to implement education policy, literally at the 'chalk face', they would be closely involved in the policy-making process. Too often, however, this is not the case and the teacher's 'voice' is often

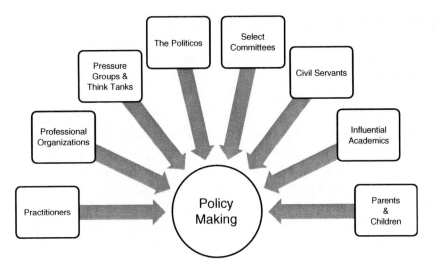

Figure 3.3 Influential Groups in the Policy Making Process

absent from policy deliberations. As Butter highlights, policy making is often a 'top-down process' with policies being imposed on teachers from above, a process that she suggests 'encourages fear and submission rather than trust and collaboration' (n.d., p. 1). Referring to the Conservative government's approach to consulting stakeholders, Bolton suggests:

> There is no crime in listening to your political friends. But a wise Government listens more widely than that, and especially to those with no political axe to grind. It is not auspicious that the formal channels of advice about education to the Government appear to be either muzzled (e.g. HMI), or packed with people likely to say whatever the Government wants to hear (i.e. the NCC and SEAC). (Bolton, 1993, p. 15, cited in Gipps, 1993, p. 11)

New Labour has, unlike the previous Conservative government, attempted to consult with a far 'broader church' (see Figure 3.3), including teacher representatives, parents and children, in an attempt to provide a 'bottom-up', more 'inclusive' policy-making process. In addition, the Treasury, particularly when Gordon Brown was Chancellor, has also assumed a central role in the policy-making process. However, only certain types of policy making have actually been inclusive, and as Larsen *et al.* (2006) point out, New Labour only tends to consult a wide range of stakeholders when the implementation of a policy is dependent on their support and cooperation. When implementing more 'cost intensive and politically or ideologically driven policies' (i.e. when the Treasury is involved), even the more 'powerful' stakeholders are not consulted and parliamentary debate and opposition are generally ignored (ibid., pp. 645–6). Thus, for example, in developing its 2002 review of child-care provision (see Chapter 4), the government consulted widely, both within and outside government, but because of the huge financial implications of the strategy, the final decisions about the government's approach to child care were made by the Treasury. As Larsen *et al.*, conclude, 'The major factors influencing the policy style of the New Labour government are thus the power relations between government and stakeholders and the type of policy under consideration' (2006, p. 647).

Select Committees

Since 1979, parliamentary analysis and reports on the functioning of government departments and their policies have been the responsibility of the government's cross-party Select Committees. Currently, the Children, Schools and Families Committee covers the work of the Department for Children, Schools and Families (DCSF) and related bodies such as Ofsted, while the Business, Innovation and Skills Committee deals with issues relating to higher and further education, that come under the aegis of the Department for Business, Innovation and Skills (BIS). While the formal role of the Select Committees is narrow, as McFall (2009) points out, in practice they have a wider remit and often embark on wide-ranging inquiries into specific issues in which they can call on the expertise and advice of relevant stakeholders and academics. This, McFall suggests, gives them 'considerable power to set the agenda for public policy':

> The power of a Select Committee lies not in an ability to make direct changes to laws, but in the capacity to get to the heart of important issues, to hold the government to account, and to speak with a credible, coherent and non-partisan voice. Ultimately, in order to influence policy, a Select Committee must command the respect of Parliament and the public. (McFall, 2009)

Ideological Perspectives

From an educational perspective, an ideology can be defined as 'any package of educational ideas held by a group of people about formal arrangements for education' (Matheson, 2008, p. 21). Thus,

> An ideology is a framework of values, ideas and beliefs about the way society is and should be organised and about how resources should be allocated to achieve what is desired. This framework acts as a guide and justification for behaviour. (Trowler, 2003, p. 103, adapted from Hartley, 1983, pp. 26–7)

Ideologies work at different levels within an education system, from informing education acts at a national level to influencing classroom practices at a local level (ibid.). There are a number of competing ideologies evident within contemporary British policy making, and some are more general, *political* ideologies (see Table 3.1), while others are more specifically *educational* (see Table 3.2). According to Trowler, 'ideology does place limits on thinking. It defines what the important questions are, where the priorities lie, how issues should be viewed, and indicates the sorts of actions that can and should be taken' (2003, p. 171).

Table 3.1 Political Ideologies

Political Ideology		
Neoliberalism	**Neo-Conservative**	**Social Democracy**
• Belief in the Free Market • Limited government intervention • Individualism • Freedom of choice	• Belief in traditions and customs • Strong state – providing direction • Central control • Disciplined society	• Belief in state intervention • Private and charitable organizations used to complement the state's activities • Pluralistic decision making • Regulation to overcome social disadvantage
For Education		
• Competition between schools • Diversity of schooling • Parental choice	• Compulsory attendance • Centralized curriculum • Traditional subjects • Focus on school discipline	• Focus on the link between education and national performance • Promotion of social justice • State intervention to mitigate the effects of multiple disadvantages

Adapted from Trowler 2003, pp. 104–18.

Table 3.2 Educational Ideologies

Educational Ideology			
Traditionalism	**Progressivism**	**Enterprise**	**Social Reconstruction**
• Disciplinary and subject knowledge • Traditions and heritage • Elitism • Teacher-centred learning	• Student centred learning • Freedom of choice for students • Subject and disciplinary knowledge not important • Mass access to higher education	• Students viewed as future workers • Emphasis on usefulness of the curriculum • Emphasis on use of new technologies and approaches • Concentration on core skills	• Education viewed as a force for social change • Radical approach to enterprise • Experiential learning • Focus on subjects • Students become autonomous learners facilitated by teachers
Has links with a Neo-Conservative ideology	**Has links with a Social Democratic ideology**	**Has links with a Neoliberal ideological perspective**	**This perspective is not evident in government policy making but is proposed by radical left-wing academics**

Adapted from Trowler 2003, pp. 104–18.

As Trowler indicates, thinking about education is always inherently ideologically laden. However, the link between ideology and education policy is not always straightforward, with governments often adopting contradictory ideological stances, or, as we shall see in the case of New Labour, trying to move beyond traditional ideological boundaries.

New Labour's 'Third Way'

The previous Conservative government was characterized by Margaret Thatcher's 'New Right' ideology, a coalition of Neoliberals (interested in free markets, competition and the control of public spending) and Conservatives (interested in preserving traditional values and authority) (Tomlinson, 2005, p. 29). When New Labour came to power it adopted what it termed a 'Third Way' approach to policy making. In essence, the Third Way is a 'middle way' or 'centrist' approach (one that has been adopted by other national governments, including the former Clinton administration in the United States) which contains elements of both Neoliberalism and social democracy; stressing the advancement and use of technology, education and competitive mechanisms to achieve economic success. In adopting such a stance, New Labour tried to distance itself from the old traditional, socialist ideology of previous Labour governments and also from Margaret Thatcher's new Right Liberalism. However, its stance is, according to Trowler (2003), inherently ideological, despite its claims to be beyond ideological imperatives:

> It is about traditional values in a changed world. And it draws vitality from uniting the two great streams of left-of-centre thought – democratic socialism and liberalism – whose divorce this century did so much to weaken progressive politics across the West. Liberals asserted the primacy of individual liberty in the market economy; social democrats promised social justice with the state as its main agent. (Blair, 1988, p.1 cited in Leathwood and Hayton, 2002, p. 139)

Discourses

According to Sutton, 'a discourse is a configuration of ideas which provide the threads from which ideologies are woven' (1999, p. 6) and can relate either to particular ways of thinking about an issue, for example, a scientific discourse, or to the kind of language that is employed in the policy-making process. Often, therefore, this results in 'labelling' being used to highlight how certain groups of individuals are viewed within the policy context. For example, labelling certain groups of boys as 'failing boys' within a policy context provides justification for the actions and initiatives that are to be put in place to ameliorate the situation and to prevent them from failing in the future. Discourses within policies are also often used to legitimize particular ways of viewing situations and thus, as a result, 'become part of the everyday discourse . . . [often excluding] other possible ways of conceptualising the nature of education' (Trowler, 2003, p. 132). For example, Trowler highlights the fact that within the policy agenda for Higher Education, the discourse

> frames the higher education system as a market catering to students as customers, situates knowledge as a commodity to be acquired and accumulated like any other and positions learning as involving the serial acquisition of learning outcomes, all available on the open market. (ibid.)

This discourse, Trowler suggests, has clearly been adopted in some of the everyday discourses that affect the way lecturers and students view education, and also in practices, such as 'credit accumulation' and 'skills audits' (ibid.). Adoption of the dominant discourse, however, is not inevitable, for although some individuals are 'captured' by it, Trowler suggests there are always others who will act in ways that subvert the message.

An Economistic Discourse

As we mentioned earlier, the economic crisis in the 1970s brought the education system under ever-growing scrutiny. One influential journal of the time, the *Critical Quarterly*, produced a series of 'Black Papers' (in contrast to government White Papers) that focused on developments in education and, in particular, on what its authors viewed as the failures of comprehensive education and the excesses of progressive educational methods. According to Ball (2006), the Black Papers established a *discourse of derision* in which education was considered to be in crisis and, as a consequence, schools and teachers were held partly responsible for the nation's economic decline. In particular, there was a view that comprehensive schooling, progressive methods, poor teaching and subversive, left-wing teachers were contributing to a decline in educational standards as well as standards of discipline and behaviour in schools, and consequently to an increase in social disorder. This 'discourse of derision' was 'legitimized' by James Callaghan's Ruskin speech in 1976 which initiated the 'Great Debate' on education.

Since then, this 'economistic' discourse has come to dominate education policy making (Tett, 2008). Education is increasingly being couched in economic terms, particularly with respect to its contribution to the nation's global competitiveness. Tett, however, highlights the fact that this 'transformation of social problems into economic problems is achieved through the emphasis on individual responsibilities' (2008, p. 1). Individuals, as a consequence, have to take the blame for any failures. The key 'social actors' in education policy – the schools, children, parents and teachers – are, therefore, all individually held responsible for the nation's economic prosperity and failure is 'blamed' on their attributes. Thus, we have the 'badly managed school', the 'ineffective teacher', the 'pupil lacking in motivation or ability' and the 'bad parent' who, according to Coles, does 'not take their responsibilities seriously enough' (2006, p. 20).

> The use of highly selective globalisation theory and informational capitalism enabled the Government to re-imagine education and so change its ecology. The aim and the effect was to alter the process of teaching and learning, the nature of institutions, the role of teachers and the place of education in society. (Porter, 2009, p. 292)

Schools and Teachers, Derision and Redemption

Prior to the 1970s, schools and teachers were generally held in high regard within society. However, from the 1970s, and certainly until the 1990s, schools and teachers were portrayed in an increasingly negative way (Hansen, 2009). As Rea and Weiner point out, 'to suggest that the poor performance of a minority of the teaching force is a main cause [of Britain's economic decline] is clearly untenable, but this is one perspective that is currently receiving wide support' (1997, p. 5). Contemporary educational policy discourse, therefore, has continued to adopt a 'shame and blame' discourse (ibid., p. 4). The 'derision' of failing schools and teachers has led to an increasing number of schools being 'named and shamed' for failing to meet the government's targets and opened up the potential for individual teachers to be demonized in a similar fashion in the future. In 1999, for example, Chris Woodhead, the then Chief Inspector of Schools, released the infamous 15, 000 statistic, suggesting that there were literally thousands of incompetent teachers within our schools. However, as Nash points out,

> [although] just 10 teachers have been struck off from their positions in the decade since Woodhead's numerical misdiagnosis. [The media] imply that this figure results from systematic failure, caused partly by the shortage of cases referred to the GTC, partly by the fact that so few of such cases have been removed, not, under any circumstances, because the discredited 15K statistic was a spectacular exaggeration. (2009)

The government has attempted to ameliorate this situation through the application of various policy initiatives in order to provide schools with the mechanism for the 'redemption' of such failings and the opportunity for 'salvation.' A new discourse of 'redemption and salvation' has, therefore, emerged:

> Competence, achievement, deliverance and salvation are promised to present-day teachers who are 'named and blamed' for the failings of decades of inadequate education recipes and policies . . . [and] because of the mass of new legislation and statutory duties, all of which require surveillance and inspection . . . it has become overwhelmingly compelling for teachers to be 'born again.' (Rea and Weiner, 1997, p. 5)

The media image of teachers and the teaching profession has, however, improved over recent years. According to Hansen, research has shown that since the 1990s, although there have been a number of individual high-profile media cases of 'bad teachers' (mainly relating to sex offences), teachers were 'increasingly being portrayed in a way which implied respectability and esteem which afforded recognition to their claims and which recognised their plight and (sometimes) beleaguered situation as a genuine problem requiring political action' (2009, p. 345).

The Child as Redemptive Agent

There are numerous, diverse and contrasting views of the child, particularly with respect to the provision of education and care, which have been subject to change over time. In the 1960s, for example, the dominant discourse with respect to the need to provide education and care for children, particularly those in need, was that of the 'deprived' child, that is, a child whose normal development was impeded by the adverse social conditions in which they lived. In the 1970s, the notion of the deprived child was replaced by that of the 'vulnerable' child, a child threatened by abuse, both from within and outside the family. By the 1980s and

1990s, the notion of the 'market child' dominated, a child whose future, for good or ill, was shaped by their parents' choice of school. A more contemporary discourse hails the 'distributed' child, a child that is dependent upon integrated public services for the maintenance of their well-being and safe keeping (see Barron *et al.*, 2007).

A construction of the child, however, that has pervaded New Labour thinking and policy making is one of the child as a 'redemptive agent'. A discourse of 'redemption and salvation' has been adopted (from which a similar discourse relating to schools and teachers emerges), in which the child is viewed as an individual who 'is not reasonable, capable and competent, but who – with proper care and nurturing can be saved' (Popkewitz, 1998, p. 25, cited in Cohen *et al.*, 2004, p. 38). There is a belief, therefore, that early childhood interventions can provide a form of 'cure' for a whole host of societal problems and save the child from 'an adult future shaped by community disadvantage and inadequate parenting' (ibid., p. 38). Indeed, according to Lister, a new paradigm is emerging in which children are regarded as 'becomings' rather than 'beings' (2006, p. 315). By investing in the provision of education and care, particularly for the most disadvantaged children, the State is simply making a social investment in children who are 'becoming' the 'citizen workers of the future' – a move that represents a shift towards a social investment model of welfare provision (ibid.).

In sharp contrast, however, the government's Children and Young People's Unit has also promoted an alternative discourse which promotes the notion of the 'autonomous child', an individual in their own right whose views should be heard within policy making. Government policy, however, has in reality tended to ignore this viewpoint and, predicated on the notion of the child as a 'redemptive agent', has fostered a managerial approach to both child care and education, based on prescription, standards, assessment and outcomes in order to achieve its objectives. As Prout suggests, as a consequence, 'despite the recognition of children in their own right, public policy and practice is marked by an intensification of control, regulation, and surveillance of children' (2000, p. 304).

Parents as Partners

Prior to the 1989 Children's Act, parents were assumed to have certain 'rights' with respect to their children. The Children's Act, however, replaced those rights with the notion of 'responsibility'. Under the act, parents had to ensure that their children were 'safe, healthy, educated and cared for' (Yeo and Lovell, 2002, p. 104). However, in line with the then Conservative government's particular ideological perspective, support for traditional family values was also set against a minimal role for the state (Murphy, 2008). Alongside parental responsibility, the Conservative government's market ideology also introduced the notion of 'parents as consumers'. Parental choice over their children's schooling was seen as a mechanism for driving up standards in schools and promoting excellence. However, as Ball and Vincent (2005) highlight, parental choice is complex – a mixture of emotional and practical concerns (see Chapter 5).

Although the state has generally been loath to become involved in family affairs, from the late 1960s parental involvement with the state, through involvement in their children's schooling, became a central tenet of educational policy. Parents were expected to become actively involved in preparing their children for school and facilitating their children's educational success. The Plowden Report (1967) highlighted the impacts of socioeconomic factors on educational success and thus 'created a deficit model of parenting', arguing for 'the greater involvement of parents in schools in order to compensate for "society"' (Muschamp *et al.*, 2007, p. 3, plus references). While this deficit model of parenting has persisted, it is gradually being replaced by the notion of 'a good enough parent' who produces 'good enough children', a notion that acknowledges the realities of family life and the various pressures and demands that contemporary society places on parents. Better, or 'authoritative', parents are viewed to be those who have high-level expectations of their children and who exercise supervision and discipline while remaining sensitive and supportive of their children's needs (Gutman *et al.*, 2009).

As a market ideology has entered education and care, parental choice has become paramount to the success of the system. Parents under New Labour, however, have been promoted as 'partners' with the state in providing for the care and education of their children, rather than as simple consumers of its products. As such, 'a notion of a home–school alliance that promotes the wider interests of children and the community' has arisen (Wolfendale and Topping 1995, p. 2, cited in Muschamp *et al.*, 2007, p. 3). New Labour, therefore, in line with other Westernized governments, has taken on a greater role for the state in ensuring that families undertake 'proper childrearing' and that their children are well prepared for school and for their future role within society. They have done so because they believe that governments have 'a legitimate and active role to play in assisting rational parent-citizens to do the best they can by their children' (Nichols *et al.,* 2009, p. 65). This approach, typically, has been characterized by intervention and regulation, particularly when parents are viewed as problematic.

Activity 3.1

Collect examples from the media of newspaper headlines and articles that provide evidence of how children, parents, teachers and schools are represented. How similar are such representations to the dominant discourses promulgated by politicians? Do you think they represent accurate or distorted views of reality? What do you consider the negative effects of such labels to be?

Research Evidence

Under Margaret Thatcher's Conservative government there was, according to Gipps, a 'hostile policy climate for research in general and education in particular' (1993, p. 3). There was a general move away from discussions with stakeholders and the use of research evidence to inform policy making towards a situation in which 'principles and gut reaction' characterized an 'impoverished policy process' guided by 'think tanks' and favoured advisors (ibid., p. 8). In addition, research evidence, even internationally renowned research, was in the main ignored. There was according to Whitty (2006a, p. 161) a perception, fuelled by the media, that educational research was generally:

- lacking in rigour
- incoherent, inaccessible and poorly disseminated
- ideologically biased
- lacking in relevance to schools
- lacking the involvement of teachers
- not cost effective.

As a consequence, one of the persistent issues for researchers has been that such views, however unfounded, have been difficult to dispel.

When New Labour came to power, it claimed to put an end to the kind of ideologically driven policy making that had been a characteristic of the previous government, pledging, in their 1999 White Paper 'Modernising Government', to use research evidence in the policy-making process. Over the last decade there has, therefore, been an increasing emphasis on evidence-based policy making, coupled with a mantra of 'what matters is what works'. According to Ozga (2004), because New Labour's policy making is no longer bound by ideological constraints, policy makers have to rely on the 'best' research evidence in order to identify 'what works' in a particular context. Research evidence also has to support the improvements that are needed in the performance of the educational system, in the face of international comparisons and competition within a global economic market.

New Labour's evidence-based policy-making approach has brought with it more resources for research and has also led to the establishment of a number of research programmes and centres, for example, the Centre for the Economics of Education and the Teaching and Learning Research Programme. In addition, there have also been long-term reviews of educational research, such as those carried out by the Evidence for Policy and Practice Information and Coordinating Centre (EPPI).

The way that research evidence is used in policy making is, however, complex, and Nutley *et al.* (2004) identify a number of ways in which research findings can be used:

- *The Political Model.* Research is used to defend a political position. For example, the use of research evidence to support a proposal to reduce class size in New Labour's 1997 Manifesto.
- *The Engineering Model.* Favoured by New Labour, in which research evidence provides the hard data on which decisions can be made, in some cases irrespective of the quality of that research. For example, New Labour's use of evidence from the Specialist Schools Trust to support the case for specialist schools in its 2001 White Paper, 'Schools Achieving Success'.

- *The Enlightenment Model.* Research findings do not directly inform policy, but the concepts and perspectives they provide pervade the policy makers' thinking. For example, research on formative assessment and assessment for learning informed New Labour thinking in this regard, which in turn is represented in aspects of the Secondary National Strategy.
- *The Interactive Model.* Research findings are only one part of the evidence on which the policy is based; the views of a wide range of stakeholders are also sought. For example, the development of New Labour's Sure Start Local Programmes.

(Nutley *et al.*, 2004, p. 30, after Weiss, 1979. See also Whitty, 2006a, pp. 165–70)

As we can see from the examples, New Labour has actually used research very selectively and, despite its claims to evidence-based policy making, has often ignored research evidence altogether. As Lawton suggests, 'Research evidence as well as the views of educational theorists have too often been ignored in favour of the quick-fix bright ideas of spin doctors and advisers at No 10' (2005, p. 142, cited in Whitty, 2006a, p. 168).

Continuity or Change?

The Conservative Legacy

When the Conservatives under Margaret Thatcher came to power in 1979, education was not a main priority, but it was becoming open to influence from some powerful groups (see Table 3.3). Conservative policies emphasized 'the use of markets and free enterprise to produce and distribute, with a minimum of regulation, the goods and services wanted by consumers' (Tomlinson, 2005, p. 31). Education, like other State services, was, therefore, viewed as a commodity and pupils and parents acted as consumers in the 'education market'. The consequence of such a policy direction was the loss of the once democratically controlled education system, and its replacement by one that was centrally controlled and funded (ibid.).

The Conservatives' ambition, therefore, was to change the whole educational system, based on a view of the existing educational system that characterized it as:

- having low standards
- having incompetent teachers
- having poor pupil behaviour – 'blackboard jungles'
- being under the 'cocoon of the welfare state' which discouraged effort.

The Conservatives' ambitious reform agenda was to be achieved through a long-term strategy that included:

- parental choice
- government control over the curriculum and assessment
- removing or reducing the powers of LEAs, teachers and their trainers
- increasing accountability
- encouraging selection under the auspices of diversity. (See Tomlinson, 2005)

Table 3.3 Summary of Some of the Key Conservative Policy Initiatives 1979–1997

Issue	Conservative Policy 1979–1997
Selection	**Education Act 1979** • Halted the Comprehensive Schools programme • Local education authorities could retain grammar schools and selection
Private Schools & Parental Preference	**Education Act 1980** – Strategies to ration educational opportunities • Protection & enhancement of private schooling • LEAs to assist pupils to go to private schools on a means-tested basis • Parental preference for schools • School governing bodies established with parental representation • Discretionary, but not compulsory, education for the under 5s • Abolition of free school milk
Special Education	**The Education Act (Special Education) 1981** followed on from the Warnock Report of 1980. Introduced the concept of special educational needs and inclusion
School Governance	Governing bodies became the major agency running schools • Increased parental influence in schools
Centralization	• Control of education became more centralized • Government took over functions normally carried out by LEAs and teachers – finance, curriculum, and examination
Removal of Teacher Autonomy	• Government took control of teachers and teacher training and introduced prescribed training courses and the control of teacher salaries • 1980 – introduced a core curriculum
Vocational Education	• The New Training Initiative 1981 (DoE) • Creation of City Technology Colleges
Wide-Ranging Reform	**The Education Reform Act 1988** • National Curriculum • National tests at 7, 11, and 14 • Local management of school budgets (LMS) • Parental choice • Opting out (grant-maintained schools) • City Technology Colleges • Ofsted – a new inspection regime for schools
Further & Higher Education	**Further & Higher Education Act 1992** Funding mechanisms. Polytechnics became universities. Expansion of HE but more control
More Wide-Ranging Reforms	**Education Act 1993** • Increase in the number of GM schools • Established funding agency for schools • Code of practice for SEN • Clarification of procedures for failing schools • Established PRUs
Teacher Training	**Education Act 1994** • Teacher Training Agency (TTA) established – more government control over Teacher Training – school based training introduced
14–19	• Plethora of youth training schemes but no coherent package • TVEI programmes in schools tried to bridge the gap • Dearing Report 1996 – called for a national framework of qualifications

Table 3.3 Cont'd

Failing Schools	• Individual schools demonized as 'failing' – Zero tolerance of such schools
	• Criteria for failure and Special Measures to deal with it
Other Policies	• Student Loans Company established to provide government funding for HE and also allowed banks, etc., to finance student loans but not fees
	• Clarification of stages of education
	• Increased provision for under 5s and excluded pupils
	• Nursery Voucher Scheme
	• Code of Practice for Schools and SENCOs established

New Labour

When New Labour came into power it was trying to shed its 'militant, cloth-cap' image. According to Tomlinson (2005), Labour showed a mixture of despair and admiration for Tory policies and took them over, reworked them or actually extended them (see also Hill, 2001). Uncharacteristically, therefore, it set out to capture the middle ground of politics, focusing on raising standards in partnership with teachers, parents and local government and promoting choice and the market while also, contradictorily, being aware of inequalities. Examining New Labour's policy initiatives in its first term of office, Leathwood and Hayton (2002,139) suggest that rather than offering something radically different there was actually a great deal of continuity between New Labour's policies and those of the previous Conservative government (see Table 3.4).

Table 3.4 Continuity and Change

Continuity with the Conservatives	New Directions
• Operation of Market Forces in education – competition between schools for pupils	• Higher levels of public spending on education
• Parental choice	• More emphasis on inclusion and social justice
• The National Curriculum and a focus on the 'basics'	• Greater emphasis on partnerships and collaboration
• Accountability	• Greater emphasis on early years education and care
• Focus on standards – testing and assessment	• Reduced class sizes
• Naming, shaming, & closing	• Expansion of further and higher education
• Focus on use of information technology	• Privatization
	• Use of paraprofessionals in the classroom

Activity 3.2: Continuity or Change?

As you read through the following chapters that relate to New Labour's policy agenda make a note of the policies and initiatives that are continuations of Conservative policies and those that are genuinely new. Overall, do you consider the New Labour government's approach to be radically different from that of its predecessor or merely 'more of the same'?

The New Coalition Government's Emergent Policies

After 13 years of New Labour government, the general election on 6 May 2010 eventually resulted in the formation of a coalition government of Conservatives and Liberal Democrats. With respect to education, one of the first things that the new Secretary of State, Michael Gove, did was to rename the DCSF the Department for Education. Included in their 'Programme for Government' released on 20 May, they highlighted their plans for families and children, schools and universities and further education, which include (see Gillard 2010 for commentary):

- Giving parents more powers to choose a good school for their child
- Better assessment of special educational needs and the removal of the bias towards inclusion
- Premiums for pupils from disadvantaged areas
- Giving teachers and head teachers more powers to enforce school discipline and to tackle bullying
- Sure Start to be retained with a focus on early intervention and with more Sure Start health visitors
- Teachers pay and conditions to be reformed with schools being given greater freedom to determine such things locally
- Improve teacher training with expansion of Teach First and a new Teach Now programme
- Simplification of regulation of standards. Inspections focused on "failure"
- More Academies and new "Free Schools" to be formed
- Further reforms of the National Curriculum. Synthetic phonics to be taught in all primary schools
- A more flexible exam system
- Reform of league tables.

Again, the continuities and changes with previous government policies are plain to see.

Summary

Education policy making in the UK has become increasingly politicized, particularly over the past 30 years. Both the Conservative government from 1979 to 1997 and the New Labour government of 1997 to 2010 have introduced what can almost be described as an 'epidemic' of reforms. Modern policy making can be viewed as a rational process, through which political solutions to contemporary issues are met, influenced by a range of stakeholders, research evidence, international comparisons, ideological perspectives, and contemporary discourses. However, policy making is seldom a rational process and the impacts of policies often vary considerably from what was originally envisaged. Conservative policy making was predicated on a Neoliberal/Conservative ideology. Such an ideology promoted a 'market economy' in education with a focus on standards driven by parental choice and centralized government control over the curriculum, coupled with a regime of assessment and testing together with the rigorous inspection of schools and teachers. New Labour's approach has followed a more centrist policy agenda that it promotes as being 'beyond ideological' boundaries, relying more heavily on research evidence than its predecessor. However, in reality, New Labour policies have often been extensions of the previous Conservative government's marketization and competition agenda, but with a greater emphasis on social inclusion, partnerships, the early years and privatization.

It will be interesting to see how education fares under the new Coalition government. There are, however, rumblings of concern over some of the policies that they have already started to implement. As Gillard (2010, p. 144) comments, 'If Gove gets his way – and there is every indication that he will – will a recognisable state system of education exist five years from now?' Only time will tell.

Useful References

Ball, S. J. (2008), *The Education Debate*. Bristol, UK: Policy Press.

Trowler, P. (2003), *Education Policy*, 2nd edn. (The Gildredge Social Policy Series). London: Routledge.

Useful Websites

w ww.fabians.org.uk The UK's leading centre-left Think Tank.

www.nationalschool.gov.uk/policyhub/ Website developed by the Government Social Research Unit.

www.policyexchange.org.uk/ The UK's leading centre-right Think Tank.

4

Caring For and Educating Children

Introduction

Children, particularly very young children, require the support and care of adults in order to thrive and prosper. The responsibility for their health, physical and cognitive development, early socialization, education and safe keeping has traditionally lain with the family. The prevalence and persistence of the notion of a traditional nuclear family consisting of a male 'breadwinner' and a female 'care giver' who provide the love, care and support for their off-spring's successful growth and development is testament to a long-held societal view that 'parents bring up children' and that parents, and in particular (as the old adage states), mothers, 'know what is best'.

One consequence of this notion, of the 'primacy' of the family in providing for the needs of their children, particularly for the very young, was a conviction that any state provision of care and education should not seek to 'usurp' that parental role (Kamerman, 2006). While most parents were happy to relinquish the role of educating their children to the State when compulsory elementary education was introduced, mothers, in particular, were reluctant to relinquish their caring roles in a similar fashion. The state, too, was reluctant to intervene, recognizing the 'privacy of the family as an institution' except where 'families . . . failed in their duty of care' (Baldock *et al.*, 2009, p. 48) and children were viewed as 'needy' as a result of neglect or abuse. Thus, even in the 1960s there was little state involvement in the provision of child care, and later in the 1970s and 1980s any provision remained targeted at the 'not normal family' (Moss, 2003, p. 27).

Child care, therefore, remained a private responsibility (Cohen *et al.*, 2004) and as Moss highlights, although '"child care" is all the rage today . . . for many years . . . [it was] surrounded by public and private hostility or, at least ambivalence' (2003, p. 25). This ambivalence was further exacerbated by a traditional dichotomy in terms of governmental responsibility for the delivery of education and social care between different government departments and different groups of professionals. Anning (2006) suggests that a legacy of this ambivalence and lack of integration has been a disparate range of social care and educational services, particularly for very young children, that is extremely fragmented and lacking in cohesion and coordination.

Education and Care: 1997 – The Context for Change

Prior to 1997, under the Conservative government, policy relating to children's education was well developed but had become highly politicized. Child-care policy, on the other hand, was largely neglected. To many, 'the very term "child care" [had] a dispiriting and dutiful heaviness hanging over it . . . as short on colour and incisiveness as the business of negotiating the wet curb with the pushchair' (Riley, 1983, in Brannen, 1998, p. 3, cited in Ball and Vincent, 2005, p. 558). As Cohen *et al.* point out:

> By 1997 . . . a system of services had evolved in England that was both diverse and fragmented. Some services were open all day, some part of the day; some took all ages up to five years of age, others took narrower age ranges, some focused on providing 'child care for working parents', others on 'education', a few on family support; some were free, others relied entirely on parental fees; some were publicly funded, others privately provided, on either a profit or a non profit basis. Some were the responsibility of the welfare system . . . others were the responsibility of the education system, local education authorities and school boards of governors. (2004, p. 52)

At the time, the responsibility for school-age and some preschool educational provision rested with the government department responsible for education – the Department for Education and Employment (DfEE). Children's education was delivered by highly trained teachers – graduate professionals, with a single qualification, a relatively high social status and a high rate of pay. On the other hand, the responsibility for child care, in its various forms, resided with the Department of Health (DoH). Such child-care services included those for very young children, that is, day nurseries, play-schools, kindergartens and childminders, and those for school-aged children, namely, holiday clubs and out-of-school activities. This diversity of provision was delivered by a highly gendered workforce with a range of competency-based qualifications, low status and low levels of pay (Baldock *et al.*, 2009).

Despite its ambivalence, the Conservative government finally succumbed to pressure to act on early childhood education and care and, in 1996, its Nursery and Grant-Maintained Schools Act introduced universal, part-time nursery provision for all 4- to –5-year-olds.

Child-care provision, however, was to be highly marketized, with a heavy reliance on a mixed market economy of State, private and voluntary sector provision. Parental choice and the market were driven by the introduction of Nursery Vouchers, which parents could use to purchase child care. The result was the growth of private child care and education bolstered by State subsidies. An unexpected consequence of the initiative was the unofficial lowering of the school starting age to 4, as many primary schools increased their nursery provision in order to take advantage of the additional funding, in what Wadsworth and George term a 'dash for cash' (2009, p. 309). Many women, however, particularly working-class women and those from certain ethnic groups, continued to distrust formal child care, preferring, as they still do, to rely on informal child care provided by grandparents and other relatives (Ball and Vincent, 2005, p. 564).

Drivers for Change

When New Labour came into power in 1997, there was a general political consensus that child care was struggling and in need of reform as a result of a general lack of investment, a lack of available places and an 'uneven patchwork' of provision (Penn, 2007, p. 194). Kamerman (2006) suggests that the factors that were providing the impetus for change were not necessarily unique to the English context; however, as Cohen *et al.* point out, the reform process that took place 'inherited a very particular demographic, economic and political context' (2004, p. 51).

A Declining Child Population

Although the population of England was not in decline, fertility rates, as in other European countries, had been declining for a number of years. In part, this was a result of women choosing to have fewer children and also to have them later in life; but it was also a result of more women choosing not to have any children at all. There was, therefore, a predicted decline in the child population (Cohen *et al.*, 2004) which, it was felt, could impact negatively on the level of need for children's services in the future.

Increasing Family Diversity

There was also a growing complexity in the range and form of care networks that families utilized. By the late 1990s, both demographic and social change had had a huge impact upon the function and structure of families in England (Muschamp *et al.*, 2007). Those traditional bastions, the nuclear and extended family forms, were in decline, a decline that was accompanied by an increasing diversification in family forms. Marriage rates had fallen, divorce was on the increase, more couples were cohabiting and the number of lone parents was growing. In addition, there was also a rise in family separations, the growth of step families, visiting families (where care for the children is divided between the parents while the children reside with one parent in the family home and visit the other) and so-called 'nesting' families (where the children reside in the family home and the parents take turns visiting in order to take care of them). As a consequence, as Baldock *et al.* suggest, 'many children's care arrangements involve a number of different settings and individuals, are vulnerable to breakdown and deny the child the coherence and consistency of care' (2009, p. 54).

High Levels of Child Poverty

One of the key drivers for reform and the policy direction it took was the high level of child poverty that existed in England. The United Nations Human Poverty Index indicated that England, with nearly a third of young children living in poverty, had the third highest level of child poverty among members of the Organisation for Economic Co-operation and Development (OECD) (UN Development Programme 2003, cited in Cohen *et al.*, 2004, p. 22). In fact, England was viewed by some as a 'serious contender for the title of the worst place in Europe to be a child' (Micklewright and Stewart, 2003, p. 23, cited in Lister, 2006, p. 21). The high levels of child poverty were considered to be a result of the 'market-driven economic strategies and low investment in education, health and welfare for children' (Baldock *et al.*, 2009, p. 80) that had been a characteristic of the previous Conservative government's approach. The negative impacts of childhood poverty on a whole host of factors, including the child's future health, development, academic achievement and general well-being, together with their future behaviours and employability, were well documented (UNICEF, 2007, p. 41). Baldock *et al.* suggest that 'the current government [saw] the reduction of child poverty as a key factor in improving educational standards and creating a better workforce and in reducing social inclusion, crime and anti-social behaviour' (2009, p. 51). As the then chancellor Gordon Brown suggested, 'tackling child poverty is the best anti-drugs, anti-crime, anti-deprivation policy for our country' (cited in Lister, 2006, p. 317).

Women's Participation in the Labour Market

Although the child population was in decline, there was, conversely, a growing demand for child care as a result of more women joining the labour market. Most of this growing demand, however, came from middle-class women who were entering or re-entering the workforce. Lone mothers and women with low educational achievement were, however, less likely to be employed, particularly full time, and as a consequence, were less likely to use formal child care, relying heavily on informal care provided by relatives (Moss, 2006). The government viewed such women as a drain on the economy, with £5 billion a year being lost as a result of women staying at home to look after their children (Alderson, 2007). The benefit culture in which they existed was seen as perpetuating a cycle of 'poverty and dysfunctionality' (Penn, 2007). Penn, however, points out that the government felt that through intervention 'it would be possible to change the attitudes and aspirations of mothers when children were very young, so that they had a more positive and proactive approach to becoming wage earners, and more vigorous expectations about their children's ability to perform well at school' (2007, p. 196, citing Glass, 1999).

Research Evidence

A growing public awareness of the benefits of early years education and care was also fuelling the demand for preschool education and care. This increasing awareness was in part due to need, but was also due to a growing body of research evidence that highlighted the benefits of preschool education not only for the child, but also for the nation's future economic prosperity. This desire to make young children 'school ready' was also driven by a governmental imperative to improve school performance at the primary level, partly in response to national concerns about standards but also in response to international comparisons of educational performance in maths, science and literacy provided by the PISA, TIMSS and PIRLS comparative studies (Taggart *et al.*, 2007).

Academic research had a crucial influence on the reform process because it provided an independent evidence base that was vital for gaining the support for, and approval of, a number of early years education and child-care initiatives. Importantly, given the Treasury's dominant role in policy making in this area, by stressing the long-term economic benefits of providing integrated care and education for children, it also provided the justification for increased expenditure on child care. However, as Melhuish (2007, p. 2) suggests, the evidence from research was 'largely overlooked' when programmes were actually designed.

Influential evidence came from a variety of projects, research studies and government reports, particularly from the United States which had a longer tradition of early-intervention initiatives (e.g. Head Start 1998, High Scope/Perry Preschool Project 2000, Chicago Child Parent Centers 2001), but also from the UK (e.g. the Rumbold Report 1990, Start Right Report 1994, EPPE 1996–2008, NESS 2001, Laming Report 2003; ibid.). Research evidence from Europe, however, was largely ignored (Rüling, 2008).

Such studies provided the government with clear evidence of the lasting and worthwhile benefits of high-quality, early-intervention and preschool education, particularly for disadvantaged children, their families, and communities. Some studies also highlighted the benefits of preschool education on success at the primary level or called for more investment in preschool education, while others supported the need for a more integrated approach in the provision of services for young children (see Melhuish, 2007 for more details).

The Organisation for Economic Cooperation and Development (OECD) provides governments with international reports and advice that relate to a variety of policy contexts. Two such OECD reports are considered models of early childhood care and education. The first, *Starting Strong* (2000 and 2006), stressed the benefits of high-quality early education for children's well-being and proposed a Nordic model of child care with universal, free provision for all young children. However, such a model came with the need for very high levels of state investment. The report also highlighted the danger of increased social stratification if a policy of promoting private-sector provision was adopted.

In contrast, the OECD's report *Babies and Bosses* (2004) proposed that the main rationale for investment in child care should be to enable women with young children to participate in the labour market. As a consequence, it suggested, governments would benefit due to greater tax revenues and reduced welfare payments. The report also proposed the use of child-care tax credits for working mothers, which could be used to encourage women to work and also to 'stimulate the private market to meet the demand for child care' (Penn, 2007, p. 193). It was the presumption of this latter report that was to have the greatest influence on government thinking.

According to Mahon, there was, therefore, 'a growing chorus of experts arguing that early childhood education and care is necessary to lay the foundations for subsequent "life-long" skill acquisition, a requisite for effective participation in the emergent knowledge-based economy and society' (2001, p. 4). However, as Murphy *et al.* point out, although the research highlighted the benefits of early years care and education it did not provide the kind of evidence needed to support the provision of full-time child care that would be necessary to enable women to fully participate in the labour market (2008, p. 135), or if it did, the government chose to ignore it (Penn, 2007).

Significant Events

The first 'Children's Charter', an act to prevent cruelty to children, was passed in 1889; however, the systems that successive governments have put in place since then to help prevent child abuse within the family have generally had failings that have, sadly, led to the loss of young lives in terrible and tragic circumstances. Such tragedies, what Baldock *et al.* call 'significant events' (2009, p. 58), have generally provided the stimulus for policy reform and have thus played a major part in influencing and shaping legislation. In particular, the tragic deaths of Victoria Climbié, Jessica Chapman and Holly Wells were influential in shaping New Labour's child-care policies. However, to this day, as the tragic death of Baby Peter and the shocking case of child abuse at the Little Teds Nursery highlight, such interventions, even the most recent ones, seem to have done little to prevent such tragedies from occurring.

Alternative Approaches to Child Care

There are a number of different models of the way in which the state can organize child-care provision. Da Roit and Sabatinelli (2007) highlight a number of different typologies of child-care models, including that of Anttonen and Sipila (1996), which suggests the following typical approaches to child-care provision dependent upon ideological perspective:

- *Social Democratic Model.* Typical of Nordic countries and characterized by
  - gender equality with high levels of female participation in the labour market
  - high levels of child-care provision
  - high levels of public subsidy and control over child care
  - high-quality provision.

- *Conservative Bismarkian Welfare State Model.* With variations to be found in France and Germany:
  - France. Monetary support is provided for child care, together with state provision in the form of écoles maternelles, almost-universal nursery education 'that cater for children aged 3 to 5'. There is also state funding and provision for children aged 0 to 2.
  - Germany. Monetary support is provided for child care but private rather than public-sector provision is promoted.
- *Familist or Traditional Care Model.* Typical of Southern European countries such as Italy, where the notion of the 'male breadwinner' is still dominant and women are encouraged to stay at home and care for their children. In such countries there is a growing private-sector provision to cater to the demand for child care.
- *Liberal Model.* Traditionally, the model adopted by the UK, which is characterized by a belief in the family as the main provider of care for children, but with targeted provision for children whose families are viewed as socially or economically deprived. There was also a heavy reliance on private-sector provision of child care.

Policies and Initiatives

When New Labour came into power in 1997, as we have seen, the stage was set for change and major reforms were on the agenda. The previous Conservative government had adopted a policy of 'benign neglect' with respect to child care; however, with the change of government, 'for the first time in peacetime, child care became a recognised policy priority alongside education' (Cohen *et al.,* 2004, p. 53). For New Labour, early childhood education and care provided a unique platform for the development of policies and initiatives that enabled government to reshape services so that they would be more flexible and responsive and also so that they could be targeted at other agenda areas such as:

- eradicating child poverty
- increasing social inclusion
- raising standards in education
- helping women back to work
- modelling good practice in child rearing for 'needy' parents
- providing children with the necessary prerequisites for a successful education. (See Ball and Vincent, 2005, p. 558)

New Labour's child-care agenda, therefore, has been predicated on a desire to eradicate poverty, improve educational standards and enhance employment opportunities, particularly for lone mothers. It has also been predicated on notions of a mixed-market economy of private and State provision, of parental choice, of support for parents to carry out their parenting roles and increasingly of universal rather than targeted provision. Importantly, it has also been based on a desire to provide an integrated approach to service provision (Cohen *et al.,* 2004).

However, New Labour has also chosen to move away from the more traditional, liberal approach to child-care provision. Its adoption of a more social-democratic approach has resulted in an expansion in the provision of child care, and the targeting of children and families living in very deprived areas, by making child care more readily available (Sure Start and Children's Centres) and more affordable through a system of tax credits. Rather than pursuing a truly social-democratic model, the New Labour government was loath to raise taxes to fund the expansion and consequently remained heavily reliant on the private sector. New Labour thus attempted to pursue a policy that seemed 'to ameliorate the worst effects of laissez-faire economic policies in the most vulnerable groups' (Baldock *et al.*, 2009, p. 52). In addition, it also pursued 'gender sameness' within policy, with policies designed to enable women to work through the provision of 'nonparental' child care together with financial support (Mahon, 2001, p. 5). However, as New Labour moved towards a more future-orientated, social-investment state, the expansion of child-care services was based on advantages for the economy, rather than on benefits for children themselves (Baldock *et al.*, 2009). As a consequence, there was 'a plethora of policy initiatives and legislation (too many to include them all) that . . . sought to move the "early years" sector from a "patchwork quilt" to a "seamless cover" of joined up services' (Taggart *et al.*, 2007, p. 12). As Cohen *et al.* point out, 'services are expected not only to enable mothers to work but to reduce poverty by breaking a presumed "cycle of deprivation" through "early intervention" and increasing cash transfers' (2004, p. 24).

A Long-Term Strategy

Soon after New Labour came into power it announced its National Child Care Strategy (1998). The strategy was hugely influenced by the ideas of two academics, Peter Moss and Helen Penn. While pledging to eradicate child poverty by 2020 and to provide good-quality child care for all children aged 0 to 14, the government's main focus was clearly on the economy and on measures that would enable women to take up employment. The key elements of the strategy (see Baldock *et al.*, 2009 and Cohen *et al.*, 2004), therefore, included:

- Integrating education and child care – providing better-quality provision.
- Making child care more widely available and accessible by encouraging its expansion, especially in deprived areas, for example, through the Neighbourhood Nurseries Initiative.
- Making child care more affordable through the provision of tax credits to working families.
- Promoting partnerships with business and allowing the private sector to help fill the need for child care.

In 2004, the government produced a revised child-care strategy – 'Choice for Parents: The Best Start for Children: A Ten-Year Strategy for Child Care'. In it they reiterated and extended many of their earlier objectives, promising parents greater choice and flexibility together with more high-quality, affordable and appropriate child care. In addition, such child care was to be available for children up to 14 years of age. While the initial strategy had targeted provision in deprived areas, this later strategy promised a more universal, rather than targeted, provision, linked to the development of Children's Centres in every neighbourhood and the Extended Schools initiatives (Baldock *et al.*, 2009).

The Children's Plan (2007) set out another long-term, ten-year strategy to ensure that the needs of children, young people and their families were met through the provision of effective, integrated services and that the five outcomes of Every Child Matters policy were met – that is, that children should be healthy, stay safe, enjoy and achieve, make a positive contribution and achieve economic well being. As the then Secretary of State, Ed Balls announced, the plan was to enable England to become 'the best place in the world for our children and young people to grow up' (DCSF, 2009, p. 4).

A Sure Start

One of the government's first initiatives, and the 'jewel in the crown' (Frost and Parton 2009, p. 115) of its policies to combat child poverty, was the Sure Start programme (1999). In 1998, the government had ordered a Cross-Departmental Review of Services for Young People, led by the Treasury, the outcome of which was a commitment to developing services to support children, especially the under-4s and their families suffering multiple disadvantages. Critically, such services were to:

- provide integrated services in a multidisciplinary and culturally sensitive way
- provide high levels of support for families
- be community based – with parental involvement and designed to meet local needs
- be long-term, sustainable and autonomous units.

Launched in 1999, the Sure Start programme attracted £500 million of government funding in order to initially set up 250 Sure Start Local Programmes (SSLPs) by 2001. The programme drew heavily on research from the United States and the model provided by the U.S. Head Start programme; however, well-established, existing child-care traditions and examples of integrated provision in the UK were generally ignored (Wadsworth and George, 2009). The aim of the project was to enhance the health, development and future prospects of young children living in deprived communities.

Each SSLP was established to provide 'joined-up' services for children under 5 and their families, living in the most deprived areas of the UK. They brought together health, child care, education, play, parental support and home support for parents together with a range of other services such as employment and benefit advice dependent upon local, community needs. The programmes also established partnerships between health, social services, education and the private and voluntary sectors but bypassed local authority involvement. As such, the SSLPs acted as autonomous units – there was no set blueprint and therefore a diversity of models arose.

Children's Centres

The involvement of the Treasury in the establishment of the Sure Start initiative meant that a rigorous evaluation of the programme took place – the National Evaluation of Sure Start (NESS). Some of the initial findings of the evaluation indicated that the SSLPs were failing to have an impact on mothers' employment and were, therefore, failing to reach the most disadvantaged of children (Wadsworth and George, 2009), and this coupled with evidence from the EPPE project suggested that change was needed (Melhuish, 2007).

The need for change was further supported by the development of the government's 'Every Child Matters Change for Children' green paper (2003) and the subsequent Children's Act of 2004. As a consequence, in 2005, in order to mainstream the kind of work that was taking place, the SSLPs were transformed into integrated Children's Centres. There was to be a Children's Centre in every neighbourhood by 2010 providing 'holistic services' for children and families (Baldock *et al.*, 2009, p. 43). Significantly, too, control of the centres was transferred from central government to local authorities to ensure that they became part of the welfare state, and as such could not be easily eradicated by future governments (ibid.). However, as Norman Glass, the former Treasury economist and architect of Sure Start, pointed out, little if anything of the original philosophy of Sure Start remained in the reconceptualized Children's Centres but the 'brand name' (in Ball and Vincent, 2005, p. 560), and that the 'initial child centred focus [was] in danger of becoming a "New Deal" for toddlers captured by the employability agenda' (Glass, 2005 cited in Lister, 2006, p. 322).

While, as Chitty (2009) points out, many aspects of Sure Start can be viewed as a success, others like Penn suggest that Sure Start was a 'social engineering experiment' that had 'grandiose, but vague, policy aims to reduce poverty . . . [which were not] operationalised in any systematic way' (2007, p. 196). In fact, Penn goes on to suggest that there is research evidence that actually indicates that 'levels of child poverty are rising again, despite the government's efforts' (Brewer *et al.*, 2007, cited in Penn, 2007, p. 196).

Integrating Care and Education

Recognizing that the 'split between child care and education was invalid and dysfunctional' (Moss, 2006, p. 77), as part of their modernizing agenda to make government departments and services more flexible and efficient, the government moved quickly to place child care under the auspices and lead of education. Responsibility for child care, therefore, was moved from the Department of Health to the then Department for Education and Employment. The move was to prove significant, because the government's plans for integration did not stop there; gradually, therefore, a number of State services have been reorganized and coordinated around the provision of integrated, holistic services for children.

Within government, this approach has culminated in the bringing together of all services (except health) for children and their families under the auspices of the Department for Children, Schools and Families (DCSF), in the amalgamation of civil service teams working in early years in the Sure Start Unit, and in the establishment of a Children's Minister and also a Children's Commissioner for each of the UK's regions. At a local level, as a result of the Children's Act (2004), Children's Trusts, Children's Services Authorities and Safeguarding Children boards, led by a Director of Children's Services, have all been established, again to organize children's services in a coordinated and holistic fashion. In addition, there has been a new duty of cooperation between the different children's services that has been strengthened by a Common Assessment Framework for establishing children's needs, an integrated system of inspection under Ofsted and a common set of performance indicators.

Wadsworth and George suggest that while 'there have been some positive interventions . . . with integrated provision of a range of services (e.g., health care, education and welfare) being readily available through a 'one-stop shop', such interventions have 'not been pursued in a coherent and systematic way and there has been an over reliance on the private sector' (2009, p. 315).

Every Child Matters

By the end of New Labour's first term in office, concerns were being voiced about the effectiveness of inter-professional and multi-agency working, particularly among those services working to protect, or as it is now termed, safeguard, young children. These concerns were vividly highlighted by The Laming Report (2003) into the tragic death of Victoria Climbié and later by the Bichard Inquiry into the murders of Jessica Chapman and Holly Wells, which focused on safeguarding issues. Such concerns were also evident in the government's green paper 'Every Child Matters' (ECM) (2003), which outlined a series of proposals to combat such failings. Until this point, models of service provision for children had 'left different professions in charge of delivering different outcomes' for children in their care (Straker and Foster, 2009, p. 119). Like Sure Start, Every Child Matters drew heavily on an American model – the U.S. government's 'No Child Left Behind'. With the advent of Every Child Matters all agencies providing services for children would have to work together to achieve the five outcomes for children, in order to ensure that children are able to:

- be healthy
- stay safe
- enjoy and achieve
- make a positive contribution
- achieve economic well-being.

The Every Child Matters agenda underpinned the Children's Act (2004) and was taken forward through the development of:

- Children's Centres
- Extended Schools
- the reforming of the Children's Workforce.

Although multiagency, integrated working was not a new concept, as Straker and Foster suggest, 'what clearly emerges from the Every Child Matters initiative is a commitment in terms of both practice and policy to maximize integration between agencies in order to improve communication and encourage the sharing of practice' (2009, p. 121). As Roche and Tucker highlight:

> The impact of *Every Child Matters* certainly appears to be influential in terms of the way it is transforming structures and processes at both the national and local levels. *Every Child Matters* has provided government with a framework for shaping practice, particularly as it relates to multidisciplinary working and the expectations of teachers and their managers within schools to support both the preventative and protection elements of safeguarding work . . . yet at the same time this new agenda carries with it a range of problems and challenges that will need to be proactively managed. (2007, p. 221)

Some of these problems and challenges that Roche and Tucker allude to, and which we discuss later in the chapter, include:

- issues of communication and the sharing of information
- new ways of working
- changing roles, relationships and responsibilities
- a growing distrust of all people who work with young children.

Every Child?

Another criticism levelled at Every Child Matters is that within it 'not all children have the same strategic significance as future citizen worker' (Lister, 2006, p. 324, with reference to Fawcett *et al.*, 2004). Thus, disabled children, gypsy and traveller children, the children of asylum seekers, and also children in care have been 'marginalized' by the policies (ibid.). However, later initiatives such as Care Matters (2006) and Aiming High for Disabled Children (AHDC) (2007) have gone some way towards bridging the gaps in provision.

Extended Schools

According to Roche and Tucker (2007) Extended Schools represent a further development of the government's strategy to promote integrated services for children in terms of their education and care. Developed as part of the Every Child Matters agenda, Extended Schools (and their counterpart, Community Schools in Scotland) owe their origins to the development of 'Full Service Schools' in the United States during the early 1980s. In the United States, such schools aim to provide integrated health and social services within the school in order to tackle educational underachievement in disadvantaged areas. There is no one model for a Full Service School; instead, schools develop services based on local need.

In light of the success of the U.S. model, in England by 2010 all schools are now expected to be Extended Schools providing a 'core offer' of extended services to children, their families, and the community; others, it is hoped, will become 'Full Service Schools'. The core services of an Extended School include 'wraparound' child care from 8 a.m. to 6 p.m., 48 weeks a year, for primary-school-aged children, together with:

- A variety of activities, for example, study support and special-interest clubs.
- Support for parents.
- Access to specialist services such as speech and language therapy.
- Community access to facilities including adult learning and sports facilities. (Teachernet, 2009a)

Importantly, teachers do not have to deliver extended services, all the services do not have to take place on the school's premises and schools can also allow other 'partners' to provide services within the school. Roche and Tucker point to research by Wilkin *et al.* (2003) that suggests that 'specific "arenas" for the development of Extended Schools appear to be emerging . . . [with some enhancing] curriculum provision and opportunities whilst others were focusing on developing community learning and leisure facilities [and] early years wraparound care provision' (Roche and Tucker, 2004, p. 219). However, there is a danger that such activities may merely be viewed as 'add-ons', a sort of 'adult education plus' (ibid.). Some of the issues surrounding the development of Extended Schools are highlighted by Wilkin *et al.* (2003) who suggest that there are issues regarding who controls the resources, personnel and funding in an Extended School and that in some instances there can be 'resistance' to their development, where people see the provision of such services as representing a deficit model of the community in which they live or simply cling to a more traditional view of the role of the school within the community.

Youth Matters Too

The government's policies for children not only refer to the very young and children in school, but also extend to encompass youth, that is, young people aged between 13 and 19 years old. In 2005, New Labour introduced Youth Matters, which together with the White Paper, '14–19, Education and Skills' (2009), set out a series of radical proposals to shape both the curriculum and services for this age group. Under the proposals set out in Youth Matters, the outcomes of Every Child Matters are integrated into the planning and commissioning of a wide range of services for young people that include:

- Local authorities working through Children's Trusts to provide integrated activities and services for young people through the use of Extended Schools and services – to include, for example, 2 hours' access to youth groups or classes per week, volunteering opportunities, enriching opportunities and safe and enjoyable places in which young people can spend their free time.
- Access to Information, Advice and Guidance (IAG) on career choices.
- Initiatives to tackle teenage pregnancy, youth unemployment, drug misuse and youth crime. (DfES, 2005)

The Early Years Curriculum

When the Conservative government introduced its Nursery Voucher scheme it also introduced an accompanying, rather narrow set of Desirable Learning Goals, for children in their early years. This meant that teachers in reception classes not only had to deliver the National Curriculum to their school-aged children, they also had to ensure that the children undertaking nursery education met the Learning Goals. As a consequence, in 2000, as Chitty highlights, New Labour's introduction of 'the *Curriculum Guidance for the Foundation Stage* . . . met with a very favourable response from many teachers and educationalists' (2009, p. 223).

The new curriculum guidance heralded a return to an emphasis on learning through play and a greater focus on the outdoors, as the old Desirable Learning Goals were replaced by more-'child-friendly' Early Learning Goals. However, many educationalists were also critical of the fact that in reality the guidance was neither 'progressive' nor 'enlightened' (ibid.). When the Foundation Stage became part of the National Curriculum in 2002, it became more prescriptive and detailed. In 2002, the government also introduced the Birth to Three Matters Framework, developed to support professionals working with very young children. The Framework was based on four 'aspects' that highlighted the interrelationship between children's growth, their development and learning and also the environment in which they are cared for.

In 2008, The Early Years Foundation Stage (EYFS) was introduced in order to ensure that there was a consistent approach to care and education from birth to the end of the Foundation Stage, and also to ensure that children achieved the five outcomes enshrined in Every Child Matters. The EYFS was central to the government's ten-year Child Care Strategy and brought together the Birth to Three Matters Framework, the Curriculum Guidance for the Foundation Stage, and the National Standards for Under 8s Day Care and Childminding. Focusing on the stages of children's development rather than on chronological age and adopting a play-based approach to learning, the EYFS provides a statutory set of standards for all registered providers of Early Years care that relate to the development, learning and care of children from birth to 5 years old (Teachernet, 2009b; see also Chapter 6).

Activity 4.1: The American Way

Rather than a Third Way approach to child care, New Labour has been accused of adopting an American Way (Jessop, 2003). Familiarize yourself with the following U.S. government initiatives that are considered to have influenced initiatives in the UK:

- Head Start (www.acf.hhs.gov/programs/ohs/)
- No Child Left Behind (www.ed.gov/nclb/landing.jhtml)
- Full Service Schools (www.ed.gov/programs/communityschools/index.html)
- Safer Schools (www.ed.gov/nclb/freedom/safety/)

⇨

Make a list of the similarities and differences between the U.S. and UK approaches. Also, identify the positive outcomes of the American initiatives that have been used to support the development of UK policy, together with the criticisms of the American approach. Do you think that importing policy initiatives wholesale from the United States has been a good thing, or should the government have paid more attention to more European models, especially those adopted in Norway and Sweden?

Impacts

Availability, Affordability and Quality

Under New Labour, there has been considerable expansion in child-care provision; however, most of this increase has been provided by the private sector and, as a result, as Ball and Vincent (2005) point out, the private sector has been the main beneficiary. However, increasing regulation, rising costs and competition from Children's Centres have led to several large providers facing financial difficulties. It is possible that the current economic climate will actually lead to the survival of only three or four large providers, thus reducing availability and also choice.

Although there has been an increase in provision, affordability of child care is still a big issue for many parents, even with the provision of tax credits. Child-care options are often dependent upon where people live, resulting in a sort of 'post code lottery' (Murphy *et al.*, 2008). In some places, particularly in London, although there appears to be a lot of choice, in reality a lot of the child care is unaffordable and, if it is affordable, is subject to waiting lists. Despite the government's commitment, therefore, to 'a child care market in which every parent can access affordable, good quality child care' (Ball and Vincent, 2005, p. 559), for many parents, particularly those on low incomes, 'meaningful choice' is, in reality, not available.

Ensuring the quality of early years provision has been a major thrust of the policy agenda, particularly in light of the rapid expansion that has been facilitated within the sector. Research evidence (e.g. the findings of the EPPE project), however, has shown that the quality of early years provision is inextricably linked to the quality of the practitioners who deliver it, in particular, the level of qualification that they hold. The study also found that early years settings that were graduate led were the most effective, with a better quality of provision and better outcomes for the children in their care (Taggart *et al.*, 2007). Baldock *et al.* (2009, p. 58), however, highlight a number of measures the government has taken to ensure the quality of early years provision. These include not only providing financial support for enhanced training and staff development but also:

- enhanced quality control and accountability mechanisms
- improved regulatory systems under the aegis of Ofsted
- national standards
- curriculum guidance.

The early years sector has therefore been placed under the same critical gaze as the rest of the education sector and is now subject to the same rigorous standards and accountability regime in the name of quality.

The Early Years Foundation Stage

While some people have welcomed the EYFS, due to its focus on raising the standards of education and care for very young children and for its aim to ensure that children are ready to start school, it has also attracted numerous critics. For example, the media have labelled the EYFS a 'nappy curriculum' (Bingham, 2009) and soon after its inception a campaign was established that included many leading child-care experts and children's authors, because it was felt that EYFS was:

- overly prescriptive
- potentially harmful to the development of children
- a breach of the human right of parents to have their children educated in accordance with their own philosophies. (Open Eye, 2010)

In an open letter to the *Times* the group suggested that the EYFS should become voluntary rather than statutory guidance, in order to give validity to alternative educational philosophies, insisting that

> Parents should have the right to choose how their pre-school children are cared for and educated. Young children should also have the right to be protected from an imposed system which harnesses their development to prescribed targets, and which may well force them into inappropriate early learning. (Open Eye in the *Times*, 24 July 2008)

Parents and their Children

It is evident that the reforms have brought benefits and changes for children and their families especially since they have brought children's issues to the forefront of government policy. However, there have also been concerns about some of the directions that the policies have taken and their agenda, in terms of the views of children and their parents that they promote. Policies, for example, on the one hand can be seen to 'invest' in children's futures, but on the other they serve to 'regulate' and control them and their parents (Lister, 2006, p. 315). According to Lister, there has been a 'strong whiff of authoritarianism about the reforms' that has been made 'to ensure that parents (typically mothers) turn their children into responsible citizens' (2006, p. 326). Indeed, a sort of 'punitive culture' has emerged in which parents are fined or even sent to jail for 'failing' to attend to their children's education. Similarly, those who seek to 'cheat' the system by trying to gain unfair access to better schools are snooped on and penalized. Families are viewed simultaneously as being the main source of care for their children and on the other hand as the main reason for them failing. In addition, families are also viewed as the main source of crime and abuse for children and negative associations between family income and recorded ill health, accidents, negligence, teenage pregnancy, smoking, stress, weaker social contacts, lower educational achievement and lower aspirations being widely promoted (Alderson, 2007, p. 125).

Alderson (2007) also suggests that children's lives are being constrained by the government's policy initiatives, with children having less freedom than they did in the past. She suggests that children are viewed simultaneously as 'threatened' and 'threatening'. As a result, on the one hand all children are viewed as being at risk, and services now have to ensure that measures are taken to protect children, not only from abuse from adults (all of whom are viewed as potential threats unless they have undergone the requisite criminal records [CRB] check), but also from all potentially hazardous environments. On the other hand, adults are seen to be threatened by the behaviour of children and simple actions like playing football in the street can be viewed as a nuisance and result in an Anti-Social Behaviour Order, or ASBO. As Alderson concludes: 'Across the whole age range, government policy seeks to tame and regulate young people, preparing them for the future labour market while freeing up their parents for the current workforce' (2007, p. 126).

Professionals

Cohen *et al.* highlight the fact that one of the consequences of the division of services between care and education was an equally divided workforce, which, as we have mentioned before, was 'distinguished by levels of training, pay [and an] approach to training [that] was fundamentally different' (2004, p. 76). It is, therefore, pertinent to look separately at the impacts that the government's reforms have had on the different workforces, for while at all other levels the reforms have been focused on integration, the workforce itself still remains as deeply divided.

The Child Care Workforce

Care work has always been viewed as 'inferior' to teaching. In the main this has been due to the fact that, traditionally, the child-care workforce has been characterized by:

- low pay
- low status
- low qualification levels
- a mainly female workforce (99%) generally under 25 years old and working in the private sector. (See Baldock *et al.*, 2009 , p. 106)

When it came into power, New Labour was highly critical of the workforce, suggesting that it was failing to meet the needs of children and that many practitioners were under qualified, with candidates of the right calibre being difficult to recruit. In addition, child-care workers were not considered to be 'professionals' due to the often 'casual' nature of their work and the fact that they were viewed as having a natural predisposition to their role, which could simply be viewed as substitute mothering (Osgood, 2009).

With the government's ambitious targets for the expansion of early childhood care and education, coupled with its drive to raise the quality of such provision, there has been a focus on raising both the level of qualification and the status of the workforce (Osgood, 2009), together with a recognition that the reformed workforce would require new knowledge, skills and competencies (Roche and Tucker, 2007). In addition, evidence from research highlighted the correlation between levels of qualifications and the outcomes for children and thus the need for more staff with graduate level qualifications.

In 2005, the government established the Children's Workforce Development Council (CWDC), a nongovernmental organization tasked with developing the child-care workforce and enabling the delivery of Every Child Matters. This has led to:

- A ladder of qualifications being developed.
- The identification of a common core of skills and knowledge for all professionals working with children and young people.
- All staff in settings, including managers, to have higher qualification levels.
- The development of the 'Early Years Professional'.

The professionalisation of the early years workforce and the emergence of the Early Years Professional have, however, met with a considerable degree of controversy, in the main because it is a model of professionalism that has been imposed by the government. As Osgood points out the government's model:

> values technical competence and a narrowly defined focus upon neo-liberal principles, which can assure transparency, accountability and measurable outcomes . . . What this model obscures from view is that 'professionalism' in ECEC might exist for its own sake . . . and might expose [the] intrinsic and collective benefits of such work. (2009, p. 747)

The development of the Early Years Professional has the potential to complicate the position of the traditional Early Years Teacher. Although both the Early Years Professional and the Early Years Teacher have a similar level of qualification (Level 6), the former comes under the aegis of the CWDC while the latter under the aegis of the Teacher Development Agency (TDA) and more importantly brings with it the award of 'qualified teacher status'. Kirk and Broadhead (2007) suggest that, due to their separateness, there is the potential for inter-professional rivalry and tension, especially over roles and responsibilities when both types of professionals are employed in the same setting.

The Teaching Profession

The government's reforms, particularly Every Child Matters with its safeguarding agenda, have provided teachers with a number of challenges, demands and also expectations (Roche and Tucker, 2007). A consequence, as Kirk and Broadbent highlight, is that 'Tomorrow's teachers will . . . inhabit and expect to flourish in a very different professional world' (2007, p. 11). Linked to the broader child-care agenda, the school workforce has also been remodelled, primarily to free up teacher's timetables to enable them to respond effectively to the Every Child Matters agenda and to promote learning within the school.

As a consequence, schools have now become sites of interprofessional collaboration with teachers having to take on the role of Lead Professional, sharing information and utilizing a common assessment framework. In the classroom, teachers are no longer what Kirk and Broadhead refer to as 'solitary operators' but are engaged in professional team working with a range of other 'paraprofessionals' that includes:

- higher-level teaching assistants
- teaching assistants
- learning mentors.

As well as working with a range of support staff within the classrooms, teachers have also had to face the challenges of interprofessional and multiagency working, working with social workers and health professionals.

There are obviously potential benefits for teachers from working in such a fashion that, as Straker and Foster (2009) highlight, include improved working practices, better communication between agencies and better outcomes for children. However, there are also potential costs. In particular, as Whitty (2006c citing Adams, 2005) suggests, there are concerns that the 'unique' role of the teacher might be threatened by this new agenda, and that schools, therefore, need to ensure that their core purpose and the role of the teacher in promoting learning remains clear. In addition, the new agenda and reforms have the potential to influence and alter notions of teacher professionalism. Whitty quotes Hayes who suggests that

> In time, teachers and their professional bodies may forget that they have an educational role. Already they match the policy apologists in arguing the introduction of the wider workforce will free them up to teach. By the time the perverse consequences of this strategy have worked themselves out it will be too late. Education will have been killed in favour of flexible attendance at therapeutic learning spaces. (2006c, p. 5)

However, as Whitty also points out, the reforms that have taken place in the wider children's workforce also have the potential to facilitate teacher professionalism being reconceptualized on a far more democratic basis.

Summary

Since 1997, the government has introduced dramatic changes to the way services for the care and education of young children are delivered. The main thrust for the plethora of policy initiatives has been a desire to increase economic competitiveness not on increasing children's well-being. Initiatives have been focused on those families living in the most deprived areas and in facilitating women, particularly those demonized lone mothers, to enter into the labour market through the provision of affordable, high-quality child care. By drawing parents into a partnership with the State, the government has become engaged in a 'social engineering project' that seeks to alter parental attitudes and aspirations, in order to move them out of poverty and benefit dependency and to improve the future life chances of their children.

In order to achieve the government's aims, the private sector has been enlisted to help provide the necessary growth in provision, services have been reorganized so that practitioners work in partnership not only with parents but also with other services in an holistic and integrated way and Ofsted has been brought in to regulate services and ensure that quality is maintained. A new Early Years Foundation Stage Framework has also been implemented to ensure a consistency of children's experiences so that children can achieve the five common outcomes – which are to be happy, healthy, stay safe, enjoy learning and achieve their potential and economic well-being.

However, despite all the reforms and vast sums of money that have been invested in the initiatives there is little evidence of real success. Child poverty is on the increase, the initiatives have had little effect on employment rates in the target groups and England remains a very unequal society which is still considered to be one of the 'worst places in the world for children to grow up'. While there have been attempts to raise the status and professionalism of those working in the child-care sector, a two-tiered workforce still exists, one that is overloaded by change and initiatives, bedevilled by standards and accountability, dogged by a notion of professionalism that simply relates to competence, relentlessly scrutinized and accused of being shambolic and disorganized; yet, as Osgood suggests, simultaneously hailed as the 'saviour of the economy'.

Useful References

Baldock, P., Fitzgerald, D. and Kay, J. (2009), *Understanding Early Years Policy*. London: Sage.

Chitty, C. (2009), Education Policy in Britain, 2nd edn, chap. 10, pp. 215–30. Basingstoke: Palgrave Macmillan.

Cohen, B., Moss, P., Petrie, P. and Wallace, J. (2004), *A New Deal for Children?* Bristol: Policy Press.

Useful Websites

www.everychildmatters.gov.uk/ Website providing information and links to information on all aspects of the government's Every Child Matters agenda.

www.nationalstrategies.standards.dcsf.gov.uk/earlyyears/ Website providing information on the government's Early Years Foundation Stage Curriculum.

5

Schools

Introduction

As education became established as a human right and nations became more actively involved in educational provision, the growth of state-funded, mass education systems has eventually resulted in an increasing institutionalization of learning, with the result that schools and education systems are now a ubiquitous feature in all developed countries. As Ballantine and Spade point out, 'Schools provide the framework for meeting certain goals of society and preparing young people for future statuses and roles' (2008, p. 69). As a consequence, schools all over the world tend to share a common structure and organization, although their general ethos and character can differ widely. Thus, we will all be familiar with schools being organized on a local basis with direction from central government and led by a headteacher, with children, in uniform, organized into classes and taught by teachers who are specialists in particular subjects and with a school day organized into teaching periods defined by the ringing of a bell.

Societal views about what constitutes a 'good, quality education' tend to reside in this common concept of the school, coloured to some degree by a sort of collective memory of halcyon schooldays of the past. Eisner (2002), in the United States, terms this the 'yellow school-bus model' of education:

> Most parents and even many teachers have a yellow school-bus image when it comes to conceiving what teaching, learning and schooling should look like. The yellow school-bus is a metaphor for the model of education that they encountered and that, all too often, they wish to replicate in the

21st century. Our schools as they are now designed often tacitly encourage the re-creation of such a model. (2002, p. 583)

The resulting collective image of what a typical school should be like is appealing to both policy makers and parents alike, and, as a consequence, according to Davies, our current schools tend to owe 'more to the past than to the future' (2005, p. 101). This love affair with the traditional is clearly highlighted in the directions that policy makers have taken in trying to resolve the perceived failures of modern education systems, in particular the failure to meet the needs and aspirations of all pupils, particularly those from disadvantaged backgrounds.

The solution, as Eisner highlights, however, has not been to change the system or conceptualize schools in a different way, but to simply reinforce those traditional values – closing 'failing' schools, replacing weak leaders with the 'inspirational', enforcing discipline and uniforms and instigating relentless regimes of performance management (consisting of testing, inspection, league tables and ultimately competitive market forces) in order to raise standards. Alternative models to the traditional school are rarely considered, perhaps because the traditional school system represents one of the most cost effective ways of educating en mass and ensuring that the right for all children to attend a school near to their home and to receive an education does not remain a mere aspiration.

In England, deciding what kind of schools we need and how they can deliver the kind of quality educational experience that will meet the needs and aspirations not only of the individual pupils and their parents but also society in general has proved a challenging problem – one that over 140 years of state intervention in the education system has so far, some would consider, failed to resolve with any degree of satisfaction. In this chapter we are going to explore how the school system has developed in England and the policy rationale for those changes. What it is important for you to reflect on as we do so is how little the actual concept of 'the school' has changed.

The Development of the School System in England

There has been a long tradition of diversified educational provision in England with the state, the Church, voluntary organizations, socially minded philanthropists and private companies all playing a part. As we saw in Chapter 1, it was not until 1870 and the Foster Education Act that the foundations of the first 'national' state education system in England were laid. What church provision of schooling there was had always been patchy and in 1870, the government stepped in to fill in the gaps, with the provision of state-funded schools for the working classes in areas where there were no church schools. Following the Education Act of 1902, most faith schools were taken over by local education authorities as the state now guaranteed compulsory Christian education for all. The 1944 Education Act maintained the existing diversity of provision with faith and non-faith schools existing side by side in Local Authorities together with a growing independent, fee-paying sector (Bates and Lewis, 2009). The 1944 Education Act also introduced free secondary schooling for all and provided Local Authorities, headteachers and teachers with considerable autonomy with respect to the running of their schools.

The structure of the new State Secondary Education System was not actually prescribed in the 1944 Education Act, which simply stated that the secondary schools in a particular area should be 'sufficient in number, character and equipment to afford for all pupils opportunities for education' (Ministry of Education, 1944, cited in Chitty, 2009, p. 20). There was considerable debate about the structure of the new system, however, ultimately the notion of a single secondary school in each area was rejected in favour of a secondary education system based on 'selection by intelligence' at 11 coupled with a 'tripartite' division of secondary schools. The result, according to Chitty (2009, pp. 20–1), was a 'rigid and essentially hierarchical educational structure' consisting of:

- Fee-paying 'public schools' catering for the wealthy elite.
- Direct grant grammar schools – fee-paying schools that received a government grant in return for offering free places to local children.
- Grammar schools for the academically able.
- A small number of technical or trade schools for those pupils with 'technical' ability.
- Secondary modern schools for the 'rest'.
- A small number of all-age elementary schools which were to be gradually phased out.

By the 1960s, the fallibility of selection at 11 was beginning to be exposed and there was, particularly among Labour politicians, a desire for a more egalitarian and meritocratic educational system that would enable greater 'social mixing'. The reorganization of the old tripartite system to provide 'comprehensive' education was, therefore, designed to 'establish a school community in which pupils over the whole ability range and with different interests and backgrounds can be encouraged to mix with each other, gaining stimulus from the contacts and learning tolerance and understanding in the process' (DES, 1965, p. 18, in Chitty, 2009, p. 12).

However, as in previous legislation, Circular 10/65 which introduced the new comprehensive system did not prescribe or compel Local Authorities to implement a particular school structure. As a consequence, a number of models of comprehensive schooling were allowed to 'evolve', which included:

- schools catering to ages 11–18
- schools catering to ages 11–16 with a separate sixth form college
- a two-tier middle (8–12 or 9–13) and upper school (12/13–18).

As Wilby highlights, 'ever since comprehensive schools were established in the 1960s and 1970s . . . no government has given them wholehearted support' (2008, p. 349), nor did they go down well with some parents and Local Authorities who fought, in some cases successfully, to retain selective grammar schools. By the 1970s in particular, the public's faith in the education system had begun to decline. The introduction of comprehensive schooling coupled with progressive teaching methods was seen as contributing to a crisis in education exemplified by a general decline in educational standards and discipline in schools (Chitty, 2009).

During the Conservatives' 18 years of government from 1979 to 1997, while a state, comprehensive education system was retained, the main thrusts of their reforms were thus aimed at introducing diversity, quality, choice, autonomy and accountability into this 'failing' system. The Conservatives were committed to the notion of diversity of provision and, in particular, to the fact that education should be geared towards 'both local circumstances and individual need' (DfE, 1992, pp. 3–4, cited in Chitty, 2009, p. 55). As Chitty highlights, at this particular time the purpose of educational reform was to create 'a hierarchical system of schooling subject both to market forces and to greater control from the centre' (2009, p. 51). Conservative measures included (see Wilby, 2008, and Chitty, 2009):

- Attempts to restore grammar schools which ultimately failed due to parental resistance – although many grammar schools were retained.
- The Assisted Places Scheme – the funding of places in fee-paying schools for 'bright' pupils from disadvantaged backgrounds which ultimately proved an ineffective means of helping such children.
- City Technology Colleges – privately financed schools established in deprived urban areas where the local comprehensive schools were deemed to have failed. However, sponsors were not very forthcoming.
- Grant-Maintained School Status enabled schools to be free from Local Education Authority control through direct government financing.
- The establishment of colleges specializing in languages or technology with a degree of selective entry.

When New Labour came into power in 1997, despite the 'totemic status' of comprehensive schools among some members of the Labour Party, their failure to deliver meritocracy and greater social mobility led eventually to the announcement that 'the age of the bog-standard comprehensive was over'. According to Wilby (2008), New Labour felt that public services, like education and health, were under threat and that if they failed to improve such services they would be abandoned by the wealthy middle classes who would then demand tax rebates for services that they no longer used. Wilby suggests that New Labour felt that 'the only way to keep [the Middles Classes] in the state sector was to offer them what they would get if they went private, choice, personal service and high standards in traditional academic subjects . . . both health and education services were turned into quasi-markets with "competing providers"' (2008, p. 350).

Since 1944, successive reforms of the education system in England have pursued the notion of diversity in provision to such an extent that there is no longer a truly 'national system locally administered'. The result, as the Teacher Development Agency (TDA) (2008) point out, is that now 'there is no such thing as a typical school in England' and thus there is a diversity of schools that vary with respect to funding, admissions and in some cases the Curriculum. As Stephen Ball (2009) has often noted, the state appears to be gradually withdrawing from its role as the 'provider' of education which it so reluctantly took on in the 1870s and is assuming a new role – one in which it takes on the various mantels of funder, commissioner and monitor of the system.

The Contemporary Context

During the late 1980s and early 1990s a 'revolutionary change' swept through the English education system. The growth of and confidence in public services, like education, was coming to an end, heralding in a period of 'retrenchment and redefinition' (Bondi, 1991, p. 126). Such changes were occurring in education systems throughout the world, particularly countries like the United States where, as in England, falling birth rates, declining public confidence in education due to concerns over standards and progressive teaching methods and economic recession had brought the relationship between education and the economy into question and raised the potential for restraints on public spending in that area. The result, was a '"neo-liberal" revolt against existing public services . . . seeking to restructure them around a market model in which "consumers" chose which service to use just like when buying commercial products' (Hirsch, 2002, p. 4). This belief in the power of the market to improve public services like education was enshrined in the Conservative government's Education Reform Act of 1988. Since then, both the Conservative and New Labour governments have used a number of interlocking policy 'technologies' which together form a policy framework with respect to schools which is designed to bring about desired improvements in the system (Simkins, 2000). Three of these policy technologies that have particular relevance to our discussions are:

- *Marketization*
  - o Parental choice
  - o Diversity of schools
  - o League tables and competition
- *Managerialism*
  - o School autonomy
  - o School-based management
- *Performativity*
  - o Targets and performance-related pay.
  - (See Ozga, 2009 and also Ball, 2006; Ball, 1999, cited in Trowler, 2003, p. 37, and Chitty, 2009, p. 73)

The use of such policy technologies is not unique to the UK situation. They form what Ball (2008, p. 25) describes as a kind of 'generic, global policy ensemble' which together are part of a 'global convergence of reform strategies' that results in a 'one size fits all model of transformation and modernisation.'

Marketization

Since 1979, successive governments, both Conservative and New Labour, have introduced a 'market-orientated' philosophy to the education system. As West and Pennell (2000) highlight, so-called market reforms included the promotion of parental choice, encouraging competition between schools, introducing new types of schools and devolving budgets and the power to innovate to schools. In the market sense, therefore, schools act as the *providers* of educational services which are *consumed* by the *customers* – the parents and their children – and have to *compete* with one another to secure the funding to enable them to survive. It is suggested that such competitive *market forces* will make schools more *customer orientated* and will force schools to innovate in order to raise the standard and quality of their provision or else fail. The market, however, is not a true market, but rather a *quasi market*, because schools do not make a profit or grow to meet demands and parents do not pay for the services that they receive (ibid.).

Choice

Parental choice is a cornerstone of the market ideology. As Goldring and Phillips point out, 'one of the most important ways in which parents are involved in their children's education is through choosing the school they attend' (2008, p. 209). Strategies designed to promote parental choice, and to provide the necessary diversity in the school system to enable choice to be exercised, have now been at the heart of contemporary policy making in England for over two decades and have often been presented as some sort of 'panacea' to social and educational problems (Coldron, 2007; Ben-Porath, 2009). To some extent parents in England always had a degree of choice about where to educate their children, being able to choose between fee-paying private schooling, different types of state schools or schooling their children at home. However, the ability to educate children outside the state sector has generally been restricted to those families who had both the desire and sufficient wealth or academic resources to do so.

Within the state sector, prior to the 1980s, Local Education Authorities (LEAs) allocated children to a neighbourhood school within designated catchment areas. Parents, therefore, with children attending such schools could exercise little choice over their children's education except on faith-based grounds. Generally, if parents wanted to avoid a particular neighbourhood school they had to move into another catchment area – something that again required resources and a certain degree of familial mobility. The introduction of the 'quasi market' into education in the late 1980s, allowing parents to exercise a preference for the school they wished their children to attend regardless of its location, brought about significant 'changes in the way families regarded and used educational services' (Hirsch, 2002, p. 5). Consequently, as a report for the OECD suggests, 'the basic model of a school within the district of residence and close to the family home, sometimes with an elite private system co-existing alongside has been modified' (2006, p. 57).

Policy Goals

Although the notion of parental choice has been inherent in educational policy making for some time, its inclusion has always aroused controversy. Choice, according to Coldron (2007, p. 2), is often legitimized by suggesting that parents desire more choice or that choice is in the best interests of both parents and their children. The advocates of parental choice also highlight the fact that such initiatives can result in the achievement of a number of important policy goals that include:

- *The Personalization of Education. Parents* are 'empowered' by choice – no longer victims of a 'nanny state'. They are able to choose schools that reflect their own aspirations for the education of their children and which match their children's needs and wants.
- *The Raising of Standards.* Parents will choose the 'best' schools for their children, thus resulting in competition between schools for pupils, particularly when funding is linked to pupil numbers. Such competition will force schools to raise their standards and thus boost pupil attainment. Schools that do not adapt to the market will suffer the consequences – failing school numbers and ultimate closure.
- *The Reduction of Inequality in the System.* Choice is open to all parents to exercise and so theoretically, the breaking of the link between where a child lives and the school they attend should result in a greater social diversity in schools and provide all children with equal access to quality schooling. (See Ball, 2009; Coldron, 2007; Hirsch, 2002)

Critics of school choice policies on the other hand suggest that implicit in choice is the notion that some children will have a better educational experience than others. Not everyone is able to exercise choice or to realize their choice of the 'best school'. Ultimately, because the 'best' schools are generally oversubscribed and are not able to expand to meet demand, there will always be 'winners and losers' (Hirsch, 2002, p. 7). In addition, the critics also point out that the notion of a market is inappropriate in an educational context, tending to disadvantage families from lower socioeconomic groups and undermine the cohesion of the national system (OECD/CERI, 2006, p. 58).

Parents as Choosers

The exercise of parental choice is a complex process that is affected by a number of factors that include not only parental values and aspirations for their children but also considerations of resources (Moser, 2006, p. 1). There is strong evidence, therefore, of a link between social class and school choice. As Moser highlights:

> While market discourses suggest that the mechanism of parental choice is a force for equality because it offers choice for all, the reality is that school choice is dependent upon the amount and type of resources parents have at their disposal . . . [which] include economic and cultural capital. (2006, p. 2)

The most 'active choosers', therefore, tend to be middle-class, well-educated parents who have the resources and also confidence to secure a place at the school of their choice (Edwards, 2002). Such parents, according to Goldring and Phillips (2008), have an advantage over those from poorer backgrounds because they have the ability to 'decode' information about schools and their resources provide them with fewer market constraints and greater choice, not only between the fee-paying and state sector but also within the state sector because they can afford to travel greater distances to schools or to relocate to within the catchment areas of better schools. Parents from lower socioeconomic groups are generally disadvantaged in the exercise of school choice and in gaining access to the best schools, because such parents lack the information and resources to employ a successful choice strategy (Moser, 2006, p. 2).

It is obvious that parents will want their children to attend a school which will provide them with the best education and opportunities possible. It is not surprising, therefore, that many parents exercise choice in order to avoid an unsatisfactory neighbourhood school (Edwards, 2002). Parents choosing alternative schooling are often seeking to avoid schools with poor reputations, where, for example, the discipline is perceived to be lax, there is a perceived bullying culture or the school occupies a low position in the league tables. In contrast, the 'best' schools are often viewed as those with high academic standards with pupils who come from advantaged socioeconomic backgrounds (see Coldron, 2007).

According to Goldring and Phillips (2008, p. 13), parental choice is, therefore, based on a number of factors and the priority individual parents place upon them. For example, some parents may place a greater importance on academic success and the school's catchment area while others may consider their child's happiness and safety more important. Thus there are a number of factors that can impinge on parental choice, which include

- the academic success of the school – exam results and league tables
- the religious ethos of the school
- convenience and ease of travel to the school
- the school's facilities
- the school's reputation
- the school's characteristics, for example, neighbourhood characteristics, size and values
- safety
- the child's happiness and friendship groups. (Goldring and Phillips, 2008, p. 213–4; see also Hirsch, 2002)

Parents tend to use information gained from *Interpersonal Networks,* that is, the personal recommendations of neighbours, friends and family rather than that gained from more *Formal Networks* (e.g. league tables, Ofsted reports, open days, PTA meetings, websites, school prospectuses, newspaper articles). Research evidence has shown that these more formal networks are not widely exploited by parents – except by the more 'active choosers', with parents relying more on the local reputation of a school (ibid.).

Promoting Choice in the English Education System

In England, parental choice was extended by the Conservatives in the early 1980s in an attempt to improve the quality of educational provision through the extension of market principles to the education system. In so doing it was felt that

> Schools would learn to offer what parents wanted or would go under, with good schools driving out the bad through the power of their success in the new education marketplace. The best schools would become dynamic, distinctive and beacons of excellence. The worst would simply close as parents took their children elsewhere. (Trowler, 2003, p. 38)

The OECD identified five main policy initiatives that can be used to promote parental choice, and the Conservative government in the 1980s toyed with or implemented a combination these initiatives in their marketization strategy (see Hirsch, 2002, p. 9; Trowler, 2003, p. 39). These initiatives included:

- Toleration of privately funded schooling. Voucher systems to help parents fund private education were considered but not implemented. The Assisted Places Scheme enabled academically gifted children from poor backgrounds to attend fee-paying schools.
- More liberal admissions policies and the abolition of strict catchment areas – 'open enrollment' meant that schools had to admit pupils up to a pre-defined number and could only reject pupils who did not meet the entrance criteria or if the school had met its admissions target. Parents could also appeal if their child did not get into the school of their choice.
- Competitive admissions policies with 'money following pupils' – the majority of school funding was based on the number of pupils the school attracted, thus rewarding successful schools.
- Policies facilitating school diversity and therefore choice.
- The provision of more information for parents on which choice can be based (e.g. school league tables, Ofsted reports).

In addition, schools were opened up to parents – they were no longer barred at the school gate. As a consequence, parents were given greater access to pupil records and information about the school, more places on governing bodies and also were allowed to vote for their school to opt out of local education authority control.

Under New Labour there was a renewed commitment to policies that promoted parental choice and diversity. Although one of the first things that the government did when it came into power was to abolish the assisted places scheme, the general policy direction was similar to that of the Conservatives, with moves both to increase choice and parental voice and engagement in schools and also to regulate it (Ball, 2008, p. 129). These policy initiatives were coupled with others that aimed to promote a greater diversity of schools and to personalize education, tailoring it to suit individual pupils' needs.

The Outcomes of Choice

As Ball highlights, the outcomes of initiatives to promote parental choice, under both the Conservatives and New Labour, have been 'confusing and contradictory'. In fact, as he points out:

> In a system where many schools now control their own admissions procedures, where there are various if marginal forms of selection and where many 'good schools' have the effect of driving up house prices in their locality, choice making and getting your choice of school are different. (2008, p. 132)

Evidence from research into the effects of school choice in England has also proved contradictory. On the one hand there is some evidence to suggest that choice mechanisms that promote interschool competition and innovation do raise pupil attainment (see Gibbons *et al.*, 2006/7) while there is also evidence to demonstrate that such competition also increases inequality and segregation due to the fact that more affluent, middle-class parents are generally more able to exploit such mechanisms (see Ball, 2008). In addition, the operation of parental choice according to Martin (2009) is a possible source of disconnect between parents and their local school and, therefore, the community.

Focus on: Fair admissions?

With some state schools hugely oversubscribed, with affluent parents buying houses in the catchment areas of good schools, with schools using tests and interviews to discriminate between applicants, with Local Authorities resorting to covert surveillance techniques in order to check parents' claims of residency in a catchment area and with thousands of children denied a place at the school of their choice because of the limits on the number of places available in each school – how can the system facilitate parental choice and also provide a fair and equitable admissions process?

When schools are oversubscribed how do they select between the pupils who apply and how can schools be prevented from using unscrupulous means to select more 'desirable' pupils? The very notion of selection can often raise controversy and debate, particularly where selection by ability is concerned, although pupil ability is only one of a range of criteria that schools can use as part of the selection process.

In a study of school selection procedures under the New Labour government's Code of Practice on Fair Admissions, West *et al.* (2009 p. 12) identified the following as the most common being used in the admissions criteria of oversubscribed schools:

- in care
- sibling(s) at the school
- 'proximity rule' – distance from home to school or travel difficulties
- in the catchment area
- medical or social needs of the child
- statement of special educational needs
- child from a feeder school
- religion
- random choice – a lottery
- selection by ability or aptitude (specialist schools can select up to 10 per cent of their intake)
- fair banding (pupils take a test and are put in ability bands from which schools select a proportion from each band to ensure a spread of pupils with different abilities).

Consider:

- How 'fair' is the application of each of these criteria in determining whether a child should attend a particular school?
- Should parents' wishes about how their children are educated be taken into consideration, or take precedence in the allocation of school places?
- As Coldron (2007) highlights, is there actually sufficient diversity within the system to satisfy all parental preferences, and where it does exist do parents perceive or know that they actually have a choice or that it is available?
- Should schools still be allowed to select on ability or aptitude and if so does this constitute the end of a comprehensive ideal?

Diversity

If all schools were the same there would be no need for parents to choose between schools, so it is obvious that for choice mechanisms to operate and be effective in achieving the policy goals there must be diversity in provision within the state sector. As we have discussed before, choice and diversified provision, whether between state and independent schools or between different types of state schools, has always been a feature of the education system in England. Because of the 'homogenising pressures on state-maintained schools' the only 'radically different' types of schooling and the only 'real diversity' of provision are to be found within the independent and home schooling sectors (Coldron, 2007, p. 5). However, as Coldron points out, only a small percentage of children (8%) are educated outside the state system and so the challenge for governments has been how to introduce diversity to facilitate choice while still maintaining the quality of provision and equitable access.

Coldron (2007, p. 5) highlights a number of mechanisms that can be used to increase the diversity of provision within the state sector. Under the Conservatives these measures included:

- *Increasing Structural Diversity.* By increasing the number of different types of schools, the number of providers and the way the schools are governed, thus providing the basis for the 'quasi market' in schools (see Table 5.1). This was achieved by allowing
  - schools to 'opt out' of LEA control – grant-maintained
  - private sponsorship of state schools
  - development of independent schools funded by the state (City Technology Colleges)
- *Promoting Educational Diversity.* In general, government policies (e.g. National Curriculum, testing, league tables) tended to make schools more educationally similar. However, a number of initiatives attempted to mitigate against this trend and to provide greater educational diversity, such as:
  - Specialist Schools Programme – offering excellence in a particular subject specialism (e.g. sport, music or technology)
- *Promoting Social Inclusion and Diversity.* Through the development of fair admissions policies, although selection processes and social 'creaming' tended to mitigate against this in oversubscribed 'good' schools, relegating those from less socially advantaged backgrounds to poorer or even failing schools.

New Labour, too, sought to enhance the diversity of provision. Although once in government they quickly abolished grant-maintained schools, they also controversially failed to abolish the remaining selective grammar schools, suggesting they should remain if parents so wished. In addition, New Labour was condemning the vast majority of state comprehensive schools and, according to Chitty (2009, p. 86), were determined to 're-energize comprehensive education' and provide a greater diversity of state schools, each having an individual identity and mission. New Labour, therefore, set out to 'modernise' the system to the dismay of many of its supporters who felt that the changes it proposed would result in the death of the comprehensive ideal.

In 1998, the Excellence in Schools White Paper started the reforms with the formation of a new framework of *Community, Foundation* and *Voluntary Aided Schools*. Greater diversity was also encouraged through an extension of the previous Conservative government's Specialist Schools programme coupled with a permitted growth in the number of faith-based schools. Later, privatization initiatives added to the diversification programme with the introduction of *Academies* and later *Trust Schools* (a state-funded foundation school supported by a charitable trust made up of the school and partners. Any maintained school can become a trust school – primary, secondary or special schools).

This diversification of schools heralded in what Blair referred to as the 'post- comprehensive era', although the system still retained the 'comprehensive principle of equality of opportunity' (Glatter, 2004, p. 4, citing Blair). However, as Chitty (2008, p. 31) points out, the fact that some schools have 'the freedom to choose the pupils most likely to succeed while other have to pick up the pieces and educate the rest' has meant that diversification has resulted in a

Table 5.1 Diversity in the School System

	Type of School	Features
Mainstream State Schools • Receive funding from the Local Authority • Either the Local Authority or the governors employ the staff, own the land and building and decide upon admissions criteria • Follow the National Curriculum • Regularl inspections by Ofsted	**Community Schools**	Have strong local community links including use of facilities for community use and provision of services like child care and classes for adult learners.
	Foundation & Trust Schools	Run by the governing body and are usually owned by the governing body and a charitable foundation or a charitable trust with an outside business partner or educational charity.
	Voluntary-Aided & Voluntary Controlled Schools	Are mainly religious or 'faith' schools, although anyone can apply for a place. The charity or religious foundation owns the land and in a Voluntary-Aided School the governing body runs the school while the Local Authority runs a Voluntary Controlled School.
	Specialist Schools	Follow the National Curriculum but have focus on a particular subject area (e.g., sports, technology or visual arts)
Other State Schools With distinctive admissions and funding arrangements	**Academies**	Independently managed, all-ability schools set up by sponsors from business, faith or voluntary groups in partnership with the DCSF and the Local Authority. Together they fund the land and buildings, with the government covering the running costs.
	Free Schools	Established on the basis of parental demand. Independent, state-funded schools, established by range of proposers. Provide inclusive education. Have freedoms similar to academies.
	City Technology Colleges	Independently managed, non-fee-paying schools in urban areas for pupils of all abilities aged 11–18. Geared towards science, technology and the world of work, offering a range of vocational qualifications as well as GCSEs and A levels.
	Grammar Schools	Are able to select all or most of their pupils based on academic ability.
	Faith Schools	Are run in the same way as other state schools but their faith status may be reflected in their religious education curriculum, admissions criteria and staffing policies.
	Community and Foundation Special Schools	Cater for children with specific special educational needs.
	Maintained Boarding Schools	Offer free tuition, but charge fees for board and lodging.
Independent Schools	**Independent Schools**	Set their own curriculum and admissions policies. Funded by fees paid by parents and income from investments. Just over half have charitable status.

Visit www.direct.gov.uk/en/Parents/Schoolslearninganddevelopment/ChoosingASchool/ for more details

hierarchical rather than a pluralistic form of diversity (Glatter, 2004). As Melissa Benn comments:

> Slowly I perceived what diversity and choice really mean – a clear hierarchy of local schools. At the top private schools, then the grammars and some of the faith based comprehensives . . . then the various kinds of comprehensives that are inevitably affected by the area in which they find themselves. (2006, p. 10)

Academies

Possibly the most significant and most controversial policy (Ball, 2009) to emerge as part of New Labour's diversification agenda was the Academies Programme, launched in 2000 by David Blunkett. The programme, the brain child of Andrew Adonis, had its origins in the Charter Schools in the United States and in the Conservative government's failed City Technology Colleges (CTC) initiative – the latter being a sort of 'half-way house' between state and independent provision (Gillard, 2008, p. 11). The introduction of academies was seen as a 'radical approach' to breaking a cycle of underperformance and low expectations in failing inner city schools (Chitty, 2008, p. 26). According to Ball:

> In many respects the [academies] programme stands as a *condensate* of New Labour education policies, an experiment in and symbol of education policy beyond the welfare state and an example and indicator of more general shifts taking place in governance and regulatory structures. . . . Innovation, inclusion and regeneration are tied together in the academies rhetoric and, to some extent, at least, are realised in practice, and are intended to address local social problems and inequalities and histories of 'underachievement'. (Ball, 2008, p. 184)

Academies were initially introduced to replace failing schools in urban areas and to provide greater diversity of provision and improved educational opportunities. There was an initial target of 200 academies to be built by 2010. The schools were to be a partnership between the government and private businesses, with sponsors initially having to invest £2 million. As publicly funded independent schools, academies and their sponsors were given considerable freedom to shape their own destiny – having a unique legal status, choosing their own headteacher and most of the governors, developing their own curriculum and being able to set aside national agreements relating to the pay and conditions of the teachers and other staff that they employ, although still subject to Ofsted inspections. Academies, however, are not a 'uniform body' and there is a great deal of variation among them. As Wilby points out, 'There is no educational proposition behind them, no philosophy of how or what children should learn, no model of what a school should be like. The point of Academies is political not educational' (2009, p. 3, cited in Curtis, 2009, p. 114).

Although academies are often well received by parents and consequently oversubscribed, there is also an active and well organized resistance to their development in the form of the Anti-Academies Alliance. They have also come in for considerable criticism from academics and educational professionals. The first sponsors were bankers, entrepreneurs, business corporations and faith groups, and it was felt that they demonstrated notions of

> 'corporate responsibility' and the caring face of capitalism and of 'self made men' [*sic*] who want to 'give something back'. These hero entrepreneurs embody some of the values of New Labour: the possibility of meritocracy, of achieving individual success from modest beginnings and wealth creation from innovation and knowledge. (Ball, 2010, p. 103)

However, there was also considerable controversy and concern over the suitability of some sponsors, particularly a small number of what Gillard refers to as 'pretty crackpot extremists' (2008, p. 22) to run schools. Concerns were also raised over the powerful influence that sponsors could exert over schooling in England (see Chitty, 2009, p. 80), particularly the increasing influence of churches and other faith groups in the running of academies. Notable among these concerns have been those about Peter Vardy (the millionaire car dealer) and his Emmanuel Schools Foundation Academies' teaching of creationism and its stance on gay teachers. As Titcombe highlights:

> Much bizarre and educationally doubtful experimentation is taking place based on the whims and prejudices of sponsors, ranging from the evangelical presentation of religious mythology as historical truth and the discrediting of science, to a belief in the need to rigorously train all pupils in the practices and ethics of free market capitalism so as to properly prepare them for employment. One academy is installing a 'call centre' so that 'pupils aspirations can be raised' by training for this kind of work . . . [and] Manchester Airport, one such prospective sponsor, has overtly stated that the principle purpose of its academy will be to provide employees for the airport. (2008, p. 56)

The opposition to the academies programme has, in some areas, been quite considerable and also successful in halting the progress of some of the proposed developments. Opponents of the academies programme suggest that such schools:

- Permit private sponsors, business and religious interests to have too great an influence in the running of state education through their control of staffing, the curriculum and the school's ethos.
- Are outside local democratic oversight and accountability.
- Undermine the independent role of school governors.
- Transfer public assets (school buildings and land) into private hands.
- Take resources from other local schools which also often have to pick up, at additional expense, the rising number of pupils who are excluded from academies.
- Are not 'local schools' and they disrupt the pattern of local provision, introduce divisive competition and threaten fair admission policies through 'selection by stealth'.
- Do not offer pupils a better education than local schools – they improve their intake rather than doing better for pupils.
- Are often imposed against local wishes, in some cases replacing schools that were not failing.
- In some areas, by default, are re-introducing a two-tier education system reminiscent of the old grammar/secondary modern system. (Yarker, 2009, pp. 319–20; Gillard, 2008,p, 14; see also Powell-Davies, 2008, and Sinnott, 2008)

Since its inception the academies programme has undergone a number of changes as a consequence of lack of sponsors, rising costs and opposition. These changes, according to Ball, (2009, p. 100), have not been part of a planned reform but the result of 'muddling through and trial and error', resulting, as Beckett points out, in a situation in which 'the original academies model is sinking under its own weight and being quietly replaced with something very different' (2008, p. 8). Despite the changes to the programme there is still considerable concern about the academies programme:

> . . . their lack of accountability to the communities they serve, the dubious nature of some of their sponsors (although universities and independent schools can now be sponsors and the financial stake hold is not as high), their high rates of pupil exclusion and their patchy performance. (Gillard, 2010, p. 142)

It has come as some surprise, therefore, that the new Conservative-Liberal Coalition government has decided to continue to facilitate the development of schools as academies, although with the proviso of more inclusive admissions policies and more openness regarding exam results and performance data. As a result, the first 32 new academies (including the first primary schools to adopt academy status) opened in September 2010, and more are in the pipeline.

Focus on: Privatization and the business takeover of schools

The privatization of state education, of which academies are just one manifestation, first emerged in the 1980s under the Conservatives in the guise of CTCs and 'assisted places'. It is, according to Ball, a process of 'destatisation' in which the 'tasks and services previously undertaken by the state are now being done by various "others" in various kinds of relationships among themselves and to the state and to the remaining more traditional organisations of the public sector' (2009, p. 101). As a 'policy device' it is not an end in itself, but has become under New Labour a force for the 'modernisation' and 'transformation' of education. According to Gillard (citing Wintour, 2005) New Labour's overall aim was that 'the state should no longer be primarily a direct provider of services, but instead become a regulator and commissioner of services purchased from public, private and voluntary sectors' (2007).

According to Rikowski (2003), privatization, or what he considers a more general 'business takeover of schools', is part of a larger phenomenon occurring at both a national and an international level which involves businesses and corporations seeking to make a profit out of state enterprises. Ball and Youdall have identified two types of privatization (Youdall, 2008, p. 16):

- *Endogenous Privatization.* Concerned with making schools more 'businesslike' and includes the development of 'quasi markets', managerialism, performativity and accountability.
- *Exogenous Privatization.* Concerned with businesses being allowed to participate in the running of public services for a profit or being used to design, deliver and manage aspects of public education.

Examples of exogenous privatization under New Labour include (see Ball, 2007; Rikowski, 2003; Youdall, 2008):

- *Education Action Zones (EAZs) (1997).* Established to raise standards in deprived areas and involved business partners.
- *Private Sponsorship of and Involvement in State Schools.* For example, the academies programme and Trust Schools.

- *Outsourcing.* Including the contracting out of services like cleaning and catering to private companies to the handing over of the management of schools to private companies (e.g. Salisbury School is contracted out to Edison School Corporation – a U.S. charter school operator) and the contracting out of educational services by Local Authorities to private companies (Walsall education services to Serco).
- *Private Finance Initiatives (PFIs).* In 1997 Partnerships UK was established to facilitate the private financing of capital programmes such as school buildings or facilities such as sports halls, heating systems, ICT or catering equipment. The private company involved owns the facilities and is able to generate income from them. Perhaps the most notable of these PFIs was the ambitious Building Schools for the Future (BSF) programme which involved both public and PFI funding which aimed to rebuild or renew every secondary school in England (only to be scrapped by the new Coalition government).
- *Public Private Partnerships.* A form of PFI; for example, the involvement of Teach First, an independent charity launched in 2002 whose mission is 'to address educational disadvantage by transforming exceptional graduates into effective, inspirational teachers and leaders in all fields'.
- *The Retailing of 'Policy Solutions' and 'School Improvement' Packages to Schools*
- *Educational Consultancy*
- *Policy Entrepreneurship.* Selling educational policy overseas (particularly in developing countries) for profit – a form of policy transfer.

According to Youdall, privatization is now entrenched in the education system and for many the rhetoric of the market 'makes good sense'; however, as she also points out:

> These approaches make education a 'commodity' owned by and benefitting the individual rather than the public good that benefits the society as a whole. This conceptual shift changes fundamentally what it means for a society to educate its citizens (2008, p. 17).

Consider:

- Are there any moral or ethical reasons why you feel that private enterprise and finance should not be involved in public education?
- In the future, should private companies and individuals be allowed to actually make a profit out of the provision of state services like education?

Free Schools

In addition to inviting all schools to apply to become academies, the new Conservative–Liberal Coalition government has introduced the concept of 'Free Schools', a 'pet project' of the new Secretary of State, Michael Gove (Gillard, 2010). Such schools will be state funded and 'not for profit'. They can:

> . . . be set up by a wide range of providers, including charities, universities, businesses, educational groups, teachers and groups of parents, in response to parental demand, to improve choice and drive up standards for all young people, regardless of their background. Free Schools will provide an inclusive education to young people of all abilities, from all backgrounds, and will be clearly accountable for the outcomes they deliver. (Department for Education, 2010)

Like academies, Free Schools will not be under Local Authority control and therefore will have autonomy over staff pay and conditions, budgets, the curriculum, term times and school days.

Free Schools are another example of policy borrowing, being based on a Swedish model of schooling, which Exley and Ball suggest is based on a 'highly selective reading of outcomes and claims about the model "improving standards faster"' (2010, p. 8). Exley and Ball, however, also highlight the fact that there is evidence to suggest that the development of Free Schools in Sweden has been accompanied by some slipping of standards and also an increase in social segregation. The desire of stakeholders to embark on such a project and consequently their impact on the English education scene is yet to be seen.

League Tables

As part of the reforms that introduced parental choice and competition for pupils, schools were required to make examination results available to parents. Schools were first required to publish their examination results in the 1980s; however, it was not until the 1990s that the results were published in the press in the form of 'performance league tables' to enable parents to directly compare the 'performance' of individual schools in order to inform choice. Initially focused on secondary school performance using measures such as the percentage of students gaining A to C grades at GCSE, later measures for A levels, Key Stages 2 and 3, were included. When it became evident that such measures favoured schools with more middle-class intakes, 'value added' and later 'contextual value added' were introduced to account for pupils' prior achievements and individual school effects, such as the number of pupils taking free schools meals.

According to West and Pennell (2000; see also Leckie and Goldstein, 2009), the publication of league tables was justified in the name of 'choice' and 'accountability' and, as such, served several purposes:

- Primarily to provide parents with sufficient information on which to base their choice of schools.
- To incentivize schools to improve in order to enable them to be competitive and attract more pupils.
- To hold schools publicly accountable for their results and therefore for the quality of provision.
- To inform Ofsted inspections, self-evaluation and management processes.
- To target poorly performing schools for special attention or even closure.

With respect to parents and choice – there is evidence to suggest that less than half of parents, mainly better-educated parents, find league tables useful when choosing a school. Parents either ignore the tables or find them difficult to understand and decode (West and Pennell, 2000). There is also evidence that schools are choosing pupils rather than parents choosing schools.

With respect to schools and accountability – league tables have proved useful as the basis for Ofsted inspections and also provide a rationale for placing schools in special measures. It is evident that the competitive nature of league tables has incentivized schools to improve. However, such improvement has often been achieved through rather dubious methods such as 'cream-skimming' – selection for academic ability, complicated admissions procedures including pupil tests and parent interviews, setting, increased number of exclusions, the coaching of borderline C–D pupils, teaching to the test and either privileging academic teaching or discouraging pupils from taking difficult subjects like science.

While league tables have their critics (and indeed in some parts of the UK they have either never been used or are no longer published), it appears that in England they are here to stay. The new Coalition government has, however, pledged to reform them, and, in future, schools will have to demonstrate the progress of pupils of all abilities (Gillard, 2010), not just the most able.

Managerialism

According to Beckmann and Cooper, as part of the process of marketization there has also been an 'expansion of the new managerialism' in schools which has resulted in 'new forms of organisation and control' (2004, p. 2). Managerialism involves the use of private sector techniques in the public sector and has resulted in schools having to behave more like businesses, in charge of managing their own budgets, resources and staffing. Adopting a more businesslike approach is considered one means of making schools more efficient while at the same time raising standards. One consequence of managerialism has been a greater emphasis on the economic functions of education rather than its broader social functions (ibid.).

School Autonomy

Allen (2010) suggests that the policy of giving schools greater autonomy was predicated on the notion that it would raise standards. Since 1979, successive Conservative governments introduced reforms that sought both to increase the power of central government over the education system while simultaneously reducing the role of Local Authorities and increasing the autonomy and independence of individual schools. In 1988, the Education Reform Act introduced 'Local Management of Schools' (LMS) – taking powers away from Local Authorities and devolving the responsibility for school budgets, buildings, management and staffing to schools, the amount of autonomy varying with the type of school. With this devolution of power came a greater role for school governing bodies in the management and running of schools particularly with respect to the appointment of staff. It was felt that such autonomy would promote more efficient decision making and resource use (Allen, 2010).

Making schools more autonomous was also a key feature of New Labour's modernization reforms. In 1997, their 'Excellence in Schools' initiative promoted both school diversity and autonomy as a key means of driving up standards. In their 2000 White Paper 'Schools Achieving Success' they suggested: 'Ours is a vision of a school system which values opportunity for all, and embraces diversity and autonomy as the means to achieve it. Autonomy so that well led schools take full responsibility for their mission' (cited in Eurydice, 2007, p. 9).

While Local Authorities no longer have responsibility for the management and financing of schools, a new form of relationship between schools and Local Authorities has been developed, one in which they oversee school improvements and also admissions. However, school-based management is not a 'silver bullet that will deliver the expectations of school reform', and until recently there has been little evidence that it has had any significant impact on educational outcomes (Caldwell, 2007, pp. 8, 22).

Leadership

One of the most significant changes to have occurred as a consequence of embracing a market approach in education is in the way schools are managed, and, in particular, how the role of the headteacher has changed. The traditional view of the headteacher, before the Conservative reforms of the late 1970s, is one of a '"first amongst equals" . . . raised from the ranks and paid a bit more to coordinate the work of the school' (Hatcher, 2008, p. 1). This form of headship is characterized by Gerwitz and Ball (2000, p. 254) through a discourse of *bureau professionalism* and *welfarism*. As such, traditional leadership is characterized by a public service ethos and as a rationale, rule bound and hierarchical, with decisions based on a commitment to professional standards and values. It is also characterized by a commitment to equal opportunities, collegiality, child-centredness and supportive relationships with teachers free to exercise their professional judgements. As Gerwitz and Ball also highlight, with the Conservative's reforms came a need for a new kind of headteacher or leader, and there was, as a result, a 'concomitant exodus of pre-reform headteachers via early retirements of various kinds' (2000, pp. 255–6).

With marketization, school autonomy and a more business like approach to the running of schools came the need for a new kind of headteacher and manager whose role was to facilitate the transformation and modernization of the system. This new form of leadership is characterized by a discourse of what Gerwitz and Ball (2000, p. 256) term the *new managerialism*. Such leadership is characterized by a customer-orientated ethos, with a focus on efficiency, cost effectiveness and instrumentalism. Such leadership is more authoritarian and competitive than the old bureau professionalism. However, as Precey (2008, p. 237) suggests, for such leadership to be successful it needs to be more transformational than managerial – promoting vision, shared goals and a productive culture with a commitment to community. This new form of leadership required the 'construction of new identities' for headteachers, a process that was facilitated by the National College for School Leadership.

Developing Leaders

Until 2000, individual schools or Local Authorities provided training for school leadership and management. Such courses often varied considerably in terms of quality and content. Many universities also provided more standardized masters programmes in Educational Leadership and Management. Attendance at such programmes was usually voluntary. In 2000, Tony Blair established the *National College for School Leadership (NCSL)*, now the *National College for the Leadership of Schools and Children's Services*, which was funded by the DCSF. Its aims were:

- To provide a single national focus for school leadership development and research.
- To be a driving force for world-class leadership in our schools and the wider education service.
- To be a provider and promoter of excellence, a major resource for schools, a catalyst for innovation and a focus for national and international debate on leadership issues.

Initially the NCSL was responsible for programmes such as:

- The National Professional Qualification for Headship (NPQH) for aspiring headteachers
- Headteachers Leadership and Management Programme (HEADLAMP) for newly appointed headteachers
- Leadership programme for Serving Headteachers (LPSH) for existing headteachers

It could be argued that these developments revolutionized the development of leadership in schools. As the college developed, it introduced new programmes for Continuing Professional Development, Middle Leaders (LfTM), Bursar Development Programmes (BDP) and Leadership of Integrated Services (NPQICL). The college also provided programmes for Systems Leadership through its Consultant Leaders Programme.

In 2007, NCSL commissioned Manchester University to look at the impact of the different models of leadership. This research found that leadership was dependent on the local context. It also found that leaders needed varying structures because of the increasingly complex environments in schools. Leadership is now seen in a wider context and includes courses to develop school administrators with Certificates, Diplomas and Advanced Diplomas in School Business Management and as School Business Directors. As a consequence of these developments, leadership within schools has changed radically over the last 10 years. Leadership training now has some coherence through the NCSL and research is taking place to look at the effectiveness and the value-added nature of the programmes.

Consider:

- What are the implications for the traditional model of the 'headteacher' as a consequence of the emergence of networks and federations of schools?
- Do you consider a 'business management approach' appropriate in an educational context?

Angela Harnett

In response to the constantly changing landscape of schooling, new models and forms of leadership are emerging. Recently, what Gronn (2000, p. 334) describes as 'the new kid on the block' – the notion of *Distributed Leadership* has gained favour. In this form of leadership, responsibility for aspects of leadership is shared among individuals within a school. In addition the notion of schools as autonomous individual entities is also changing with the development of a whole range of partnerships, federations and networks of schools (as described below). New models of schooling include:

- *A Single School.* One school, one headteacher and governing body. However, there can be co-leadership that involves staff without qualified teacher status joining the leadership team.
- *A Collaboration (Soft Federation).* Formal partnership across a number of schools. May include noneducational partners.
- *A Partnership.* Groups of schools which form informal and formal agreements to work together.
- *A Federation.* Two or more schools working together under one governing body.
- *Co-location.* The school or children's centre shares a site with a school of a different type or with another service and where there is a strong link across governance, leadership and management.

As a consequence new styles of leadership, management and governance will inevitably emerge in order to accommodate these new ways of working.

The Impact on Teachers

The Terrors of Performativity

Another policy device used by both Conservative and New Labour governments to modernize schools and raise standards is 'performativity'. Performativity is concerned with accountability – a teacher's 'performance' in the classroom being measured in the 'productivity' of their pupils in the form of 'targets' determined by test scores and exam results. Teachers whose performance meets or exceeds such targets are rewarded through 'performance-related pay'. Teachers are constantly judged and measured through systems of appraisal, league tables and results, databases, inspections, peer reviews and reports in the constant drive to raise standards (Ball, 2003). Such 'tyranny', what Ball refers to as a 'system of terror' (2003, p. 49), has placed a great deal of pressure and stress on teachers and, in some cases, has shifted the emphasis in the classroom from one of creative engagement in the learning process to simply 'teaching to the test'.

Summary – Schools in the Future

Since the late 1970s, a series of radical reforms, under both Conservative and New Labour regimes, have sought to both modernize and transform the school system in England. As in other countries, a series of reform technologies has been used in the process, including competition, school diversity, parental choice, new forms of leadership and governance, privatization and entrepreneurship, league tables and performativity. Radical changes to the way that education was conceived with respect to child care, with the introduction of Every Child Matters, led to the inception of the 'extended schools' and ultimately 'full service provision', which we discussed in Chapter 4. According to Ball, the consequence of this has to be to render 'education like a commodity rather than a public good' (2008, pp. 42–3).

However, while systems and practices have been changed, have they really done anything to significantly alter the experience of schooling? As we highlighted at the start of this chapter, our vision of what constitutes quality in education still resides in the traditional model of the school. Thus, despite the reforms, the new buildings and the emergence of a new age of business and philanthropy, it could be argued that schools have changed very little indeed. As Davies highlights:

> We can see school uniforms today that would not have been out of place in 1950; plans for new schools are still dominated by rectangular classrooms of 50sqm built to contain classes of 30 children, which are segregated by age. Children still move on mass at regular intervals defined by a bell and disgorge into a maze of corridors; they are frequently segregated by something called 'ability' although the concept was denounced many years ago . . . and we still largely define success as the consequence of sitting at a small table and writing furiously for two or three hours. (2005, p. 102)

As Eisner suggests, by clinging to the traditional model of schooling, what reforms often fail to address is:

> the vision of education that serves as the ideal for both the practice of schooling and its outcomes. We are not clear about what we are after . . . [and what] . . . we want to achieve? What are our aims? What is important? What kind of educational culture do we want our children to experience? In short, what kinds of schools do we need? (2002, p. 577)

So will there ever be radical changes to the system, will truly new ways of educating children facilitated by new technologies ever emerge? Perhaps it will be 'parent power' exemplified in the new Free Schools that will actually become a new radicalizing force within education, making a 'different type of school' truly possible.

Useful References

Ball, S. J. (2008), *The Education Debate*. Bristol: Policy Press.

Chitty, C. (2009), *Education Policy in Britain,* 2nd edn. Basingstoke: Palgrave Macmillan.

Useful Websites

www.dcsf.gov.uk/performancetables/ School league tables.

www.direct.gov.uk/en/Parents/Schoolslearninganddevelopment/ChoosingASchool/DG_4016312 Government information on school choice.

www.education.gov.uk/ The Department for Education website.

www.nationalcollege.org.uk/ The National College for the Leadership of Schools and Children's Services.

LEEDS TRINITY UNIVERSITY COLLEGE

6

The Curriculum

Introduction

What did Tony Blair really mean in 1997 by his famous statement, 'Education, education, education' as Labour was entering government for the first time in years? Lawton comments that despite this vote-winning mantra, the New Labour government showed no real understanding of the purpose of education in a democratic society, partly because they 'appeared to be just as keen on choice and competition as their Thatcherite predecessors. . . . [as a consequence] The opportunity for re-thinking the National Curriculum was missed' (Lawton, 2008, p. 339). Education was viewed as important because, as Wolf highlights, 'Education is big because it is seen as the engine of economic growth, a sure-fire route to future prosperity and victory in a global competition' (2002, p. x). She goes on to make the following chilling statement, that 'an unquestioning faith in the economic benefits of education has brought with it huge amounts of wasteful government spending, attached to misguided, even pernicious policies' (ibid.). It is not surprising that politicians' accounts follow a different narrative.

David Blunkett is quoted as summing up the final years of the twentieth century as a time of 'innovation, ideas, creativity, skills and knowledge' (Blunkett, 2000, cited in Wolf, 2002, p. xi) and so we enter 'the knowledge economy'. At that time, there was considered to be a battle between countries in the 'high-skill economies or the low-skills equilibrium' (Finegold and Soskice, 1988 in Wolf, 2002, p. xii) and as such, from 1988 onwards we have witnessed a growing government interest and interference in the detail of the curriculum and its delivery, as politicians have come to see the school system as primarily a 'national investment' rather than the 'right of every child' (Kelly, 2009, p. 214).

The UK is not the only country to do this. 'In many countries the overriding policy imperative for education . . . is to help maintain a competitive economic edge' (Broadfoot, 2007, p. 31); but it is the UK that is distinguished from other developed countries' practices by the speed with which it has seized control, not only of the content of what is taught but also of the ways in which such content is delivered. As Broadfoot explains, the effect of the Conservative government's 1988 Education Reform Act was to move teachers' focus away from the needs of children and a child-centred pedagogy 'towards a preoccupation with the delivery of standardised curriculum content in increasingly prescribed ways' (2007, p. 71). Kelly goes so far as to suggest that since then we have come full circle from the 1944 Education Act 'with its promise of education for all according to age, aptitude and ability' (2009, p. 8), and furthermore, have experienced 'excessive political interference in the education system and particularly the school curriculum' (2009, p. 217). The result of this is a move towards a curriculum which is vocational 'almost to the exclusion of all other considerations of education' (2009, p. 8). This leads us to the question, what is education for? The answer from politicians today would seem to be to support economic growth, but what has happened to the other aims and purposes?

Defining Our Terms

Bartlett and Burton discuss how difficult it is to actually define the term *curriculum* and refer to Hayes's definition, 'the sum total of what pupils need to learn' (Hayes, 2006, p. 57, in Bartlett and Burton, 2007, p. 75). Kelly argues that the curriculum is a complex concept which does not just relate to the content or syllabus for any educational programme. It is also of major importance to any educational system: 'if you get the curriculum wrong, not only do academic standards fall but behaviour and attitudes deteriorate too' (Kelly, 2009, p. 217). Moreover, the curriculum has a powerful legal basis; changing it is a difficult process and takes a long time. However, it is also important to remember that the curriculum is not set in stone; it is a selection, a choice that someone has made. It is a social construction.

Kelly defines the curriculum as 'the totality of the experiences the pupil has as a result of the provision made' by any educational institution (2009, p. 9) and subdivides the whole curriculum into

- the *planned curriculum* which is delivered but which is not necessarily the same as that which is received by pupils and students;
- the *formal* taught sessions and the informal clubs and extra-curricular activities offered by teachers; and
- the *hidden curriculum* which relates back to the socializing functions of schools which were discussed by Bates and Lewis (2009).

The National Curriculum

Prior to 1988, the curriculum was regarded as the domain of the teachers and local authority advisors and was no business of central government. The curriculum was, in fact, famously referred to as '"the secret garden" not to be trodden on by politicians' (Chitty, 2005, cited in Kelly, 2009, p. 189). When the first nationalized state curriculum was introduced in the UK in 1988, through the Education Reform Act, there were clear distinctions made according to what the then government felt were the most important aspects of what schools taught, in terms of the core and foundation subjects. Lawton discusses the notions of an entitlement versus a 'straightjacket' curriculum, either of which could have emerged from the Conservative government of the time (2008, p. 338).

Following Kenneth Baker's arrival as Secretary of State for Education in 1986, what emerged was considered to be a very old-fashioned model of the curriculum. The curriculum that was selected was set out as a hierarchy of subjects with prescribed time allocations for their delivery. English, maths and science were deemed to be the core of knowledge, which the Tory government believed should be placed at the heart of children's learning in the state school system. As a consequence, nearly half of the week was devoted to these subjects. Interestingly, none of these major reforms were intended for private schools, and as Ward and Eden suggest, this was undoubtedly related to the aim of marketization of the state system: 'independent schools did not need a national curriculum because they were already in a market' (2009, p. 70). The core curriculum was followed closely by the foundation subjects, that is, courses in history and geography as separate subjects once more (despite teachers' attempts to integrate the humanities); the arts, in terms of music and art; technology and physical education; while, in secondary schools, pupils would also have to choose a modern foreign language. Information Technology was added in 1992. The whole curriculum was made up of the above along with religious education and sex education, and the later additions of cross-curricular themes and dimensions together with the informal curriculum of extra clubs, trips and events the school might offer outside formal lesson times.

A National Curriculum might have been designed very differently and more imaginatively as other writers and philosophers have had different ideas about the way knowledge could be organized. In 1977, for example, HMI published a model that they had been developing over a number of years which had divided knowledge into areas of experience, not subjects; these were

- the aesthetic and creative
- the ethical
- the linguistic
- the mathematical
- the physical
- the social and political
- the spiritual. (HMI, 1977, cited in Chitty, 2008, p. 346)

However, such ideas were ignored by the politicians and civil servants who were the authors of the Education Reform Act,

> The implementation of the legislation setting up this National Curriculum not only reflected a disregard for all research evidence, whether empirical or conceptual, but also a very positive and deliberate rejection of this, and displayed what can be described only as an anti-intellectual stance towards curriculum theory and planning. (Kelly, 2009, p. 256)

Ward and Eden (2009) point out that such a curriculum would have been very comfortable with senior Conservative politicians as it would have been what they had experienced in their public and grammar schools. 1988 also saw the introduction of further divisions between different stages of schooling. Historically, education in the UK had been split between primary and secondary phases, with the changeover occurring at 11 years of age for most children. ERA added to this by dividing children into two further phases, creating four distinct 'key stages' (KS) with legally prescribed 'programmes of study' for each stage (see Bates and Lewis, 2009, p. 66).

The stated purpose of the National Curriculum was to provide a broad and balanced education for all pupils as an entitlement and to promote all aspects of children's development while preparing them for the demands of living and working in a modern Britain. Despite this all-encompassing statement, with which few teachers could argue, it was the emphasis on linguistic and mathematical cognitive ability that many educationalists felt was a return to an almost Victorian view of the way knowledge is constructed and should be imparted. Many noticed the similarity between Baker's list of subjects and the 1902 Secondary Regulations (Lawton, 2008, p. 338). The tone of the documents justifying its introduction was overtly 'instrumental, vocational and commercial. . . . The imagery . . . is that of the marketplace, of commerce and industry. It is a factory farming view of schooling' (Kelly, 2009, p. 257). Moreover, as Chitty exclaims, 'the national curriculum quickly became a national syllabus' (2008, p. 347). It was certainly very far from the vision of a curriculum appropriate for a democratic society, put forward by Kelly, which should 'be concerned to provide a liberating experience' which promotes

> freedom and independence of thought, of social and political empowerment, of respect for the freedom of others, . . . an acceptance of variety of opinion, and of the enrichment of the life of every individual in that society, regardless of class, race or creed. (Kelly, 2009, p. 8)

The original National Curriculum has undergone numerous revisions in an attempt to make the legally prescribed subject requirements actually deliverable. This was one result of the failure of the consultation process to take teachers' and professionals' views into account. Already, in 1990, Kenneth Baker added cross-curricular themes and dimensions as something of an after-thought to the heavily subject-dominated National Curriculum in an attempt to provide something of the values that were missing from the original prescribed list of subjects. These included such areas as Economic and Industrial Understanding with the purpose of supposedly helping pupils to prepare for the opportunities and responsibilities of adult life, the emphasis being very firmly on the responsibilities.

The mode of delivery suggested for the themes was the 'permeation' model, which meant that there was no statutory content and these aspects were intended to be taught through the subjects. Initially, teachers signed up to any in-service course which contained a reference to the National Curriculum, including cross-curricular aspects, but, in practice, it was the subjects that were given teachers' attention after an initial bout of anxiety relating to attempts to make the whole package fit into an average school week. A colleague working on the Welsh theme of Community Understanding in 1990 described it as 'trying to squeeze the mortar between the bricks after the house has been built'. The themes had no real content, and, moreover, were not assessed, which led inevitably to their assuming secondary importance to the subjects. Furthermore, subject boundaries, which had been disappearing in more holistic approaches to content delivery, were fully reinstated and, moreover, the boundaries between school and nonschool knowledge were firmly reestablished (Whitty, 2002). Accordingly, this displeased both left- and right-wing politicians as the focus was very much on cognitive outcomes rather than morals and values (ibid.). However, as a result, the power which subjects hold within the British education system has never really been challenged.

The Role of the Teacher

Throughout the various forms of the National Curriculum, 1993, 2000, 2001, 2002, 2003, 2004, 2008 and 2009, the role of the teacher has remained central to curriculum implementation, whether at the micro level of lesson planning or the macro level of national developments (Kelly, 2009). For example, it was the strong opposition from teachers' unions which led to the abandoning of testing in all but the core subjects (Lawton, 2008, pp. 339–40). Although 'the professional role of the teacher has been emasculated by the centralised and detailed organisation of learning' (Pring, 2009, p. 203), the teacher has always retained some power over what is actually taught in the individual classroom; and if they do not agree with the overall educational purpose of any initiative, they are in a key position to ensure its failure unless they can be increasingly 'controlled' into compliance (Kelly, 2009, p. 16). *Enter Ofsted!*

Ofsted and the Standards Agenda

Another development from ERA was the introduction of the Office for Standards in Education, or Ofsted, whose purpose was to oversee the implementation of the National Curriculum and demand accountability from schools and individual teachers through detailed inspection visits. Kelly suggests that their activities could be likened to those of 'thought-police' – 'designed to prevent teachers from indulging in acts of "sabotage" by acting on their own professional judgements' (2009, p. 15). The government's intention was that the threat of inspection would frighten teachers into working harder, and thus drive up standards (Broadfoot, 2007). The belief was that competition would, in itself, create better schools and the publication of data would enable parents to choose the best schools, ensuring a fear of closure for schools that did not do well (ibid., p. 74). Yet, such strategies are far more about accountability of teachers and schools than actually enabling teachers to provide better learning experiences for their pupils. Despite this, 'raising standards has all too often been elevated to become *the central* objective of educational policy' (Broadfoot, 2007, p. 31) which, for many, undermines the main purposes of education (ibid). Although inspections have now changed to a 'light touch' regime, with far more emphasis on schools' self-evaluation documents, the inspection system has played its part in charting the movement from 'more indirect influences for central government on the school curriculum [to] intervention and direct control' (Kelly, 2009, p. 16), with the focus very heavily directed towards curriculum delivery. Furthermore, Ofsted has now been charged with overseeing standards at every stage of Children's Services from birth to 19 so the range of their power has been dramatically extended. An even more sinister by-product of the inspection regime, according to Kelly (2009), has been the way in which governments have been able to enforce further prescriptions of practice without resorting to legislation; simply introducing new criteria to the inspection framework has guaranteed compliance.

Approaches to Curriculum Design

As stated earlier, since 1988, the curriculum in UK schools has been dominated by subject knowledge which is assessed through a complex system of testing, the approach very much relating to education as a *product*. However, *knowledge* deemed desirable for pupils to acquire, itself a political decision, is not the only place to start when designing a whole programme of study. Planning can begin with *aims and purposes* or can be more concerned with the ways in which *the learning experiences* are to be organized (*the process model*). Each of these approaches is linked to a particular theoretical perspective and thus echoes the discussions in Bates and Lewis (2009) regarding the aims and purposes of education itself, which are then translated into a curriculum.

The government chose a National Curriculum which was, and has continued to be, content and assessment driven which translates into curriculum objectives and targets. This, in turn, means that the ideology behind it has become overtly instrumental. As such, it rules out developmental approaches to planning and the role of the teacher as curriculum developer. A clear example of government interference in issues of curriculum development and panic responses to anxiety about educational standards can be seen in the introduction of the National Strategies which provide a clear example of teachers' approaches and professional judgement being totally disregarded by politicians on both sides of the house.

Focus on: The Literacy Strategy

The National Literacy Strategy (NLS) began life as a project in the final days of the Conservative government in 1996, the purpose being to raise standards in language in primary schools. The pilot project was to run for 5 years in local authorities that had volunteered to trial it. When New Labour came into power, David Blunkett, as Secretary of State, continued with the strategy and set targets for primary schools to achieve by 2002 – 80 per cent of pupils in KS2 were to reach level 4 in literacy; however, these targets were not met.

Without waiting to see the evidence from the 5-year trial and before any evaluations were published, the NLS was implemented across the whole of the UK. The strategy set out how teachers should teach literacy in a very prescriptive manner, taking up one hour a day with teachers addressing the whole class using the infamous 'big books', thus becoming a state-enforced pedagogy. It was compulsory unless a school could demonstrate that it could do better using other methods of teaching reading.

The NFER acknowledged that while some progress was made by pupils, it was felt that this could not be sustained; however, no other methods of teaching literacy were tried out as a comparison. This begs the question that concentrating resources into one area would inevitably produce some positive results. The NLS was, in fact, based on Ofsted's very questionable pseudo-research relating to phonics. Do children learn to read by seeing the whole text and predicting meaning or do they begin with letters and sounds? (Kelly, 2009). Academic research shows it is a mixture of both.

By 2005, although the targets set by Blunkett had not been reached, the government simply continued with its commitment to synthetic phonics. In fact, some teachers were in favour of certain aspects of the NLS, but the problem remains that the NLS was presented as the *only* way to teach literacy, and took away teachers' freedom to choose different methods at different times. It was also rigidly implemented everywhere in the country and represented an approach by government officials that implied that they know better, despite their only experience of education theory and practice being their memories as pupils. This continued the theme of politicians distrusting teachers' professionalism, and it is 'the failure of politicians and administrators to listen to the professionals' which has contributed to the current 'sorry state' of the education system (Kelly, 2009, p. 217).

For their part, teachers had to deliver the NLS whether they believed in it or not. The NLS has also contributed further to the reduction of trainee teachers' ability to understand the process of teaching reading and writing – they simply follow the script. It also encouraged whole-class teaching with teachers doing much of the talking, using low-level questions to lead children to a set answer (Kassem *et al.*, 2006).

Consider:

- Did you experience the Literacy Strategy? If so, how effective did you think it was?
- Is it the role of government to impose a Strategy across the whole country, dictating to teachers how they must teach a subject?

The Literacy Strategy provides a clear example of what Kelly describes as teachers 'being told what to teach' and, following the introduction of a National Curriculum for teacher training, is also an example of how their trainers are required to train them to 'deliver' the stipulated curriculum rather than to reflect on its major feature so that questions of the purpose or justification of this curriculum, or even of its logical or intellectual coherence, have effectively been removed from their sphere of influence. (2009, p. 30)

Thus, the teacher is removed from the position of 'expert' to simply one of 'deliverer' of a curriculum that is a 'plan of action created elsewhere' (Pring, 2009, p. 203). Ward and Eden also put forward an interesting theory relating to the continuing focus on the basic skills of literacy and numeracy as stemming from New Labour's belief in their importance for working-class Britain to improve educationally and somehow recover the national position in the world economy. The national strategies 'effectively brought a return to the nineteenth century elementary school curriculum of the three R's' (2009, p. 77) but was deemed to be what the vast majority of children needed to meet industry's demands.

Assessment and the Curriculum

Why Is Assessment Important?

Assessment in some form is necessary for a variety of reasons. Educators need to be able to judge whether or not their students are making progress and whether their teaching methods are appropriate and effective. Most educational assessment is based on professional judgement and is, therefore, difficult to reduce to a kind of formulaic measurement. Yet it is precisely this form of assessment that has come to dominate the British educational system since 1988 in the form of Standardized Assessment Tasks (SATs) (which quickly became Standard Attainment Tests), a strategy borrowed from the United States. Kelly suggests that such standardized forms of assessment have served the purpose of exerting and maintaining even greater control over teachers and their practice with their mechanistic, or 'technicist', methodology (2009, p. 143).

As we have already stated, one of the main reasons why educational professionals carry out assessment is to make ongoing decisions about the success or otherwise of their teaching methods. As such, assessment is a key part of the curriculum planning process at whatever level. Such assessment can be informal or *formative* or it can generate a more formal piece of evidence at a particular point in time, known as *summative assessment;* examinations or tests, for example. A further purpose of assessment allows the teacher to diagnose what problems a student may be experiencing and to remedy this situation by adapting their practice, possibly on an individual basis. Finally, assessment generates data that can be communicated to interested parties, parents, governors and government bodies and therefore provides some evidence relating to how an individual/class/school/local authority or even the country as a whole is doing in certain aspects.

Forms of Assessment

As with approaches to curriculum design, there is an increasing number of assessment strategies being developed, the most common being

- norm-referenced
- criterion-referenced
- ipsative (measuring progress against oneself).

There has also been an interest in portfolio building which can, in fact, incorporate some of the above. There is growing evidence, however, that many forms of assessment are subject to variability; basically, even *objective* assessment is recognized as being *subjective* (see Broadfoot, 2007, p. 27).

To a certain degree, upper secondary education has always been organized around the demands of the public examination boards responsible for 16+ and 18+ qualifications, but, following the introduction of the National Curriculum, such controls were extended to primary schools as well. Other casualties of ERA included the mode three programmes that teachers had been able to develop in order to meet the needs of their particular pupils. These allowed teachers to devise the content and evaluate coursework through continuous assessment, but in the climate of distrust of professionals' judgement that followed 1988, such courses disappeared, along with subjects such as Expressive Arts and Integrated Humanities. These subjects were perceived as dangerous inventions of left-wing teachers, represented by members of the 'Rank and File' section of the National Union of Teachers.

The result has been an age of assessment-driven curricular development where data generated by constant centralized testing has become the 'currency' of the education markets (Broadfoot, 2007, p. 73). Furthermore, 'the language of standards and targets, performance indicators and strategies, evaluations and transparency is as pervasive as it is familiar' (ibid., p. 64). Assessment has, therefore, come to be used not as a means of monitoring pupils' progress but as a mechanism for monitoring the quality of teachers and the education they are providing. As a result, examination data, published in the press, can have the effect of judging and punishing certain schools without any real discussion about the social and economic context in which they might be operating.

What we have been living with for the past 20 years has been a system where 'at all levels, the testing and inspection procedures control and determine the curriculum' (Kelly, 2009, p. 150). It is certainly the case that following 1988, assessment was reduced to a simplistic, if frequent, form of testing which arose from the assumption that some forms of assessment can be neutral and objective and that the publication of league tables would provide some kind of incentive to schools 'to drive up standards' (Broadfoot, 2007, p. 65). This relates back to the point made early in this chapter that education represents a large investment and successive governments have become increasingly concerned with proving to the public that this is a worthwhile investment and at the same time allows them to appear to be 'tough' on standards.

Such a policy of combining central control of education together with a market forces ideological approach is thought to be a political vote-winner and justifies the huge financial cost of implementation and the emotional cost for teachers and pupils alike. The 'proof' placed in the public domain in the form of league tables supposedly enables parents, among others, to make comparisons regarding the quality of one school against another. It is not surprising that teachers have felt pressure to ensure their classes reach expected targets, that is, to teach to the test, as the emphasis has shifted to performativity rather than real learning. The inevitable result is that the curriculum has become narrower.

Such a simplistic concept of educational measurement is, according to Broadfoot, a myth and what is more, inhibits educational development. She also points out that there is an inherent incompatibility between the obsession with standards with its reliance on traditional forms of testing and the pursuit of a knowledge economy which supports competitiveness in the global economy of the twenty-first century (2007, p. 49). Assessment now provides a system of social organization as educational achievement often governs individual opportunity and competition has become increasingly important; you have to be the best, not just reach a standard.

After 20 years of teacher criticism, the Curriculum Council for Wales agreed to discontinue SATs in 2004 and, despite some attempts by government in England to hold on, SATs were abandoned for KS1 across the UK in 2008. Centralized testing of pupils at other key stages is to continue, even being supported by the Independent Review on Primary Education which was published in 2009, and this despite the public fiasco of the marking and publication of the KS 2 and 3 results in the recent past.

Meanwhile, Lawton described the National Curriculum in 2008 as being in a complete mess with the idea of entitlement having disappeared leaving only a 'testing regime' and league tables in England (Wales and Scotland had already abandoned them). Nevertheless, 'Successive New Labour teams have stuck with their policy of "choice" and have justified league tables in terms of providing information to parents' (Lawton, 2008, p. 340). Instead, their way of dealing with issues in the curriculum has been to make more and more subjects optional resulting in a system that is totally out of balance. The exception to this appears to be, for many writers, the re-introduction of Citizenship in the early twenty-first century as a subject in its own right. Meanwhile, Ofsted continues to wield huge power over increasing numbers of educational institutions.

Instrumentalism and the Vocational Education Response

Looking back over the 20 years it has taken for teachers' voices to be heard, we can see the increasing emphasis of marketization as the dominant educational ideology throughout the 1990s and early twenty-first century. Yet, 'the economic metaphor that schools will improve once they behave more like private profit-driven corporations and respond to the demands of "consumers" ignores critical sociological issues that make the school consumption process extremely complex' (Whitty, 2002, p. 12). For, as Whitty points out, it is inevitable that changes in schools will not in themselves change families' economic and social position. Giving parents more choice of schools, if indeed that has ever really happened, will not reverse patterns of social and cultural disadvantage. While teachers can facilitate change and development with individual children and whole groups, they cannot be held responsible for very complex patterns in society in general. Yet successive governments have relentlessly continued to blame 'poor teaching' for all society's ills, for example, the naming and shaming of supposedly 'failing schools' which has been a policy passed on from Conservatives to Labour. See Chapter 8 for a more detailed account of the changes undergone by the teaching profession whereby blame has gradually shifted from the state to the individual professional.

Vocational Education

Current drivers for the focus on vocational education under the guise of the pursuit of quality lie, first, with the increasing emphasis on international comparisons relating to educational performance following the development of what Broadfoot refers to as systems of 'categoric' assessment such as PISA providing the 'defining principle of contemporary education policy in many countries' (Broadfoot, 2007, p. 67). Second, recent economic crises have seen governments demanding ever more from their education systems in order to provide hope for the future. Third, market forces ideologies have gained dominance over educational practices and finally, the focus of policy has shifted away from discussions about inputs such as teacher (or doctor) numbers, to an obsession with outputs measured by means of targets and penalties.

UNESCO has monitored the huge increase in investment in secondary and further education around the world (see Wolf, 2002) and this, in turn, has led to a growth in the teaching profession as more students either choose, or are coerced into entering post-compulsory education. According to Wolf (2002) the investment of individuals in their own education has until now appeared to be worthwhile in that the more educated you are (no matter what subject you study) the more you are likely to earn. However, students are currently paying higher fees and face the prospect not only of postponing the start of their earning lives but, possibly, of long-term unemployment.

Such a phenomenon is not new (Wolf, 2002). Government reports going back over a hundred years have made reference to the need for a better technical education system in the UK. Yet, schemes such as the Youth Training Scheme (YTS) in 1983, which was a response to the high level of youth unemployment, and the creation of such bodies as the MSC right through to the creation of GNVQs, have failed to redress the apparent economic decline of the UK workforce in relation to comparative countries. There have, in fact, been numerous attempts to design an alternative curriculum with its own set of nationally accepted and recognized qualifications; successive governments have attempted to introduce such frameworks – Youth Opportunities Programme (YOP), Youth Training Scheme (YTS) and Technical and Vocational Educational Initiative (TVEI) to name but a few.

According to Wolf, in the UK, the term 'vocational' is usually linked to jobs that are manual, technical or even craft-based (2002, p. 58). There is also a recognized hierarchy, reflective of status which seems to be unchallenged with 'vocational' coming somewhere near the bottom of the list. In this way, Britain has always chosen a different model of vocational education to our neighbours. In mainland Europe and Scandinavia, for example, apprenticeships have remained outside government control or standardized qualifications and have continued to provide a respected route for young people into worthwhile employment.

Prior to the introduction of comprehensive schools in the UK, children were divided overtly into separate groups. Following the abandonment of the tripartite system, the model chosen for a standardized curriculum has failed to cater to the full range of pupils being educated in the same school. The curriculum has, therefore, played its part in establishing another form of tripartism through the establishment of a separate 'vocational' and less respected route for those perceived as less able. If, according to the government, economic problems were a result of an underqualified workforce, then the answer lay in the development of intermediate qualifications known, initially, as NVQs. This was the first mention of competence-based assessment, 'the ability to perform activities in the jobs within an occupation, to the standards expected in employment' (Wolf, 2002, p. 72). Skill standards became 'occupational standards' and led to an obsession with 'standards' in general.

Different lead bodies represented different industries and initially set out to write their own standards. However, these became so complicated in design, language and format that few groups were able to comply. Industry did not take up NVQs and there was still no overarching framework. Young people did not like them; instead, more and more of them wanted to do A levels. Therefore, until recently, BTEC and City and Guilds have remained the providers of vocational qualifications often customized for specific firms. However, the debates around the need for a standardized qualifications continuum continued and the 1990s saw the introduction of GNVQs which were seen as an A level for the less able.

In 2001, David Blunkett announced new plans for vocational education and insisted that vocational GCSEs were the way forward, now to be available from age 14, with a route through to vocational A levels and then higher-level apprenticeships. Subjects included Health and Social Care, Engineering, Leisure and Tourism as well as applied versions of the existing academic subjects such as Science, Business and ICT. As we can see, industry has continued to be given a position of influence over key issues of educational policy despite its own relatively poor performance. The blame for continued economic decline has remained firmly with teachers and schools for not producing workers with the right skills to keep Britain at the forefront of industrial development (Wolf, 2002, p. 105). This is linked to the continuing myths that 'the purpose of the school system is only to support the economy and that the education system is deficient' (Kelly, 2009, p. 236).

Consequently, in 2005 the QCA reviewed the secondary curriculum once more with a view to providing a greater emphasis on pupils' personal attributes and practical life skills, to reduce the prescription of content-driven academic subjects such as History and Geography and to give teachers a little more freedom over subject content in general. Similarly, a realization that a generation of children educated under the national curriculum had led to a downturn in the creative industries, just at the time when creativity and innovation were becoming skills demanded by industry, resulted in various attempts to insert a degree of creativity back into the curriculum. This included initiatives such as All Our Futures (1999), the 'Creativity Agenda' and the enormous amounts of money injected into projects run by 'Creative Partnerships'. Recent proposals and policy implementation at both primary and secondary levels have provided what New Labour believes is the answer to the problems and criticisms discussed in this chapter.

The Current Situation

The Secondary Curriculum

Following the recent review of the National Curriculum, in 2007, the Programmes of Study have been amended yet again with a view to improving coherence between subjects and reducing the overall level of prescription, in other words, something of a reversal of the policy trend of the past 20 years or more. The result is, apparently, a more flexible framework, with seven of the original 1987 subjects at KS4 now being optional (Chitty, 2008, p. 346), allowing the teacher 'more opportunity to tailor the curriculum to meet the needs of each individual student' with special attention on 'transitional material to ensure smooth progress to key stage 4 and beyond'. DCSF conferences have been held across the country and online support provided for this new Secondary National Strategy (SNS).

In 2008, the first teaching of this revised curriculum took place, together with the introduction of new diplomas in specific vocational areas. These are the latest developments in the attempt to bridge the gap between academic and vocational courses and qualifications, yet it is by no means certain that they will fare any better than their predecessors. It is also interesting that these diplomas are referred to as applied learning, not vocational. The first five were launched in 2009:

- construction and the built environment
- creative and media
- engineering
- information technology
- society, health and development.

However, as yet only a quarter of expected schools have taken them up (Baker, 2009).

Further diplomas have been added since 2009, including

- manufacturing and product design
- hospitality, catering
- business administration and finance
- hair and beauty
- environmental and land-based studies.

Other diplomas will be introduced in 2010 in the following areas:

- sport and leisure
- public services
- retail
- travel and tourism.

The first national curriculum testing of this new curriculum will be held in 2011 following the phasing in of three subjects from a more traditional academic base, Humanities, Languages and Science, the plans for which, incidentally, have not been welcomed by industry (Baker, 2009), fearing that they could distract young people from the traditional qualifications in such subjects.

A common format for each of the 17 diploma subjects is supposed to ensure that teachers will be able to make connections between subjects, emphasize the new cross-curricular dimensions and allow time and space for students and teachers to better understand the nature of their studies. Such statements appear to indicate that teachers' voices have been heard after more than 20 years, and, as the blurb on the DCSF website states, a 'coherent learning environment' will allow teachers to 'exercise their professional judgment in designing and delivering their subjects'.

All these diplomas are to sit alongside existing examination systems and therefore will not be allowed to replace the so-called gold standard of GCSEs particularly at the A level (Baker, 2009). This had been the recommendation of Mike Tomlinson, the former Chief Inspector of Schools, who had been commissioned to review the whole 14 to 19 curriculum and examination system in 2004, the result of which was keenly anticipated by the teaching profession. However, the Labour government shied away from such radical changes with diplomas, instead giving a nod in Tomlinson's direction.

Recently, new aims for the curriculum had been agreed on by educational professionals, according to government documents, and the curriculum was now to reflect a close link with the ECM outcomes. Therefore, all young people should be helped to become:

- Successful learners, who enjoy learning, make progress and achieve.
- Confident individuals who are able to lead safe, healthy and fulfilling lives.
- Responsible citizens who make a positive contribution to society. (DfES, 2003)

Schools are seen as central to ensuring young people's well-being, both physical and emotional, thus a framework for personal learning and thinking skills (PLTS) has been designed involving six skill groups. These are to enable children and young people to become

- independent enquirers
- creative thinkers
- reflective learners
- team workers
- self-managers
- effective participants.

The skills are designed to work together with two new non-statutory programmes of study for KS 3 and 4. These cover the areas of personal well-being, economic well-being and financial capability encompassing personal, social, health and economic education, sex education, careers education, enterprise, financial capability and work-related learning, linking in with programmes of Social and Emotional Aspects of Learning (SEAL) already established in many schools.

It is interesting that government rhetoric is now calling for 'passionate and committed teaching' which encourages 'open-minded investigation . . . creativity, experimentation, teamwork and performance'. Teachers are being encouraged to create real learning experiences with 'activities beyond the school'. Successful implementation will require cooperation and support from parents, the community and the ability to allow learning to take place in 'challenging and unfamiliar contexts' (QCA, 2008).

This sounds as if it is setting teachers free from the restrictions of the past, yet will be difficult to suddenly conjure up after a generation of teachers have been cowed into taking few risks in the name of accountability and 'safer schools'. The new cross-curricular dimensions may be more inclusive and imaginative than their original counterparts in 1989, namely:

- identity and cultural diversity
- healthy lifestyles
- community participation
- enterprise
- global dimension and sustainable development
- technology and the media
- creativity and critical thinking.

However, it is difficult to comprehend how teachers are going to find time to incorporate all of the above in an average school week. New approaches to assessment may well be heralded as more personalized (APP), yet experience tells us that time will inevitably be concentrated on subjects that lead to examination statistics, as long as league tables persist.

The new diplomas have cost '£65.2 million over the past three years. Over the next three years they will cost an additional £373 million. Publicity and marketing alone has cost more than £7 million over the past two years' (Baker, 2009, p. 85). The government was therefore setting great store by their success. They also demand a system of collaboration from consortia of schools and FE colleges similar to that encouraged by TVEI 20 years earlier, despite the fact that the intervening period has been one of overt competitiveness. Such cooperation may be welcomed as a 'good thing' (see Pring, 2009); however, many questions remain. Will diplomas fare any better than previous short-lived vocational qualifications such as the Certificate of Pre-Vocational Education (CPVE) or the Diploma of Vocational Education (DoVE) or be unpopular like the recently named VCEs? (Allen, 2007). The stumbling block for all previous initiatives has been the lack of parity of esteem for anything other than GCSEs and A levels with employers and, to some extent, with H.E. Interestingly, independent schools have completely ignored them, instead favouring the International Baccalaureate (IB) and the Cambridge Pre-U (Baker, 2009, p. 86).

Practical obstacles will also need to be overcome, such as the discrepancy in the pay levels between teachers in schools and FE staff, the professionals who will now be teaching increased numbers of under-16-year-olds, while in some cases possibly not being technically qualified to do so. Moreover, how will the inclusion of a younger age group affect the ethos of colleges? Training of teachers will inevitably be costly as schools struggle to provide for these new curriculum subjects, timetabling will become increasingly complex and transport of pupils between schools expensive.

Inevitably, the system of levels of diplomas has been made more complicated by the introduction of Progression and Extended Diplomas across all 17 subjects while the ever-present desire to prove parity of esteem with the A level system has led to an overcomplex and dominant grading and assessment scheme (Baker, 2009, p. 89).

Finally, all of these questions are overshadowed by the uncertainty of whether the whole system will remain in place with a change in government.

The Early Years Foundation Stage

At the other end of the age spectrum, Labour introduced a formal curriculum for those children from 0 to 5 through the introduction of its Early Years Foundation Stage in 2008. This followed earlier guidance for the Foundation Stage (QCA, 2000) and an assessment regime in the form of a profile, introduced in 2003. The EYFS is constructed under four key themes:

- A Unique Child
- Positive Relationships
- Enabling Environments
- Learning and Development.

These are supported by six curricular areas:

- Personal and Emotional Development
- Communication, Language and Literacy

- Problem solving, Reasoning and Numeracy
- Knowledge and Understanding of the World
- Physical Development
- Creative Development.

Each of these is delivered through 'planned purposeful play' with a balance of adult-led and child-initiated activities, and the whole represents the first time that the preschool learning experience has been prescribed in this way.

Interestingly, the medium of play is also being emphasized in the new primary curriculum which is being focused upon together with the six areas of learning outlined above as a way of ensuring a coherent framework for learning from 0 to 14. 'These areas of learning provide powerful opportunities for children to use and apply their knowledge and skills across subjects' (Rose, 2009, p. 12).

The Primary Reviews

In 2009, the Cambridge Primary Review, led by Professor Robin Alexander was published constituting 28 pieces of research and representing the most comprehensive review of primary education since the 1967 Plowden Report. It was based on a set of coherent aims to drive the curriculum and pedagogy and advocated testing children for the sake of their progress not for a system of national monitoring and control. The report contained the suggestion that the Foundation Stage should, in fact, be extended to 6 years of age, delaying the beginning of formal primary education by 1 year. The report furthermore contained 75 recommendations beginning with the aims which drive the curriculum, teaching, assessment and so on. It advocated getting rid of the national strategies and instead combining a national framework with a locally devised community curriculum and argued that pedagogy should be based on evidence and principle. The curriculum content should be focused around eight domains including Citizenship and Ethics and Faith and Belief and the final report included a revision of educational funding and argued for a new form of educational discourse in order to avoid repetition of the previous pattern of hastily introducing policies without a real understanding of the nature of the issue they were supposed to address. The review was welcomed by professionals but was not well received by the Labour government, sensitive to the implied criticisms of over a decade of policy initiatives. Instead they turned to the so-called Independent Review of the Primary Curriculum (Rose, 2009).

The Rose Review

The Rose Review of the primary curriculum was commissioned by the government itself and 'staffed by government-paid officers' (Richards, 2009, p. 337). It was charged with answering the basic questions of what the curriculum should contain and how it should be taught and its final report began by acknowledging the achievements of recent years brought about by the national strategies which 'must remain a priority'. The importance of subject teaching was equally upheld although there was an acknowledgement that there had been too much prescribed content and, in a reference to the Cambridge Review, an agreement that 'the curriculum is only as good as those who teach it' (2009, p. 9).

The main recommendation from the review was to retain the National Curriculum but to strengthen the links between the key stages and, in future, to review the whole curriculum at the same time. The aims and values of the recently reviewed secondary curriculum were to be extended to primary with a unified statement which incorporates the principles of Every Child Matters, the Children's Plan and the 2002 Education Act. Knowledge, skills and understanding were structured under the same six areas of learning, providing continuity from the EYFS to KS3, and this was to be supported by a framework for personal development. Phonics was to be retained as the core approach for teaching reading.

With regard to assessment, teachers were to remain responsible for KS1 in English, Maths and Science. At KS2, teacher assessment was to be combined with National Curriculum tests in English and Maths and at KS3 the eight levels were to be retained for all subjects (p. 84) 'based on the dubious notion that understanding can be "levelled"' (Richards, 2009, p. 300), although research is to continue into the validity of single-level tests.

It has been noted that the Independent Review does have some positive recommendations, for example, its recognition of the importance of oracy (Richards, 2009), drama and role-play, as well as providing a greater emphasis on personal development. However, by and large, the Independent Review has been greeted with disappointment for its failure to introduce radical change and its overall conservative approach. As Richards comments, 'it was strait-jacketed by a government-inspired brief to which it has adhered tenaciously; and it contained no direct or indirect challenge to, or questioning of, any current or past government policies' (2009, p. 299). Further criticisms include the fact that Rose has held on to the core subjects with the disproportionate amount of class time allocated to them and the continued dominance of the testing regime. While the Cambridge Review began with and grew out of clearly defined aims, the Independent Review has had aims grafted onto it, as some kind of legitimation (ibid.).

Activity 6.1

Design a curriculum which you feel is relevant for the twenty-first century; you can focus on one particular age group. Consider your starting point and which curriculum planning model will inform how you develop your ideas. Try not to be limited by current government proposals.

Summary

In this chapter we have considered the curriculum from the early days of the first ever British National Curriculum through Labour's many attempts to revise it. In 2008, Lawton pronounced that 'apart from the success of the Citizenship Curriculum, the rest of the school curriculum is now in a mess' (2008, p. 340). Similarly, Chitty observed at around the same time that early reports from the Cambridge Primary Review indicated that many children were 'in flight' from an experience of learning that they find 'unsatisfactory, unmotivating and uncomfortable' (2008, p. 346). It remains to be seen whether the latest versions of the National Curriculum really do become an entitlement for all pupils or whether they continue to operate as a 'strait-jacket' (Lawton, 2008) on teachers' professional practice, and, moreover, whether they will ever be fully implemented.

Since this chapter was written, a new government, a coalition between the Conservative and Liberal Democrat Parties, has come into power. As a result, the findings of both the reviews of primary education referred to in this chapter have been ignored and the primary curriculum remains very much as it was before. We expect to see renewed emphasis on subjects and, in some ways, a return to the spirit of 1988.

Useful References

Broadfoot, P. (2007), *An Introduction to Assessment*. London: Continuum.

Kelly, A. V. (2009), *The Curriculum Theory and Practice*, 6th edn. London: Sage.

Useful Websites

www.curriuculum.qdca.gov.uk Qualification and Curriculum Development Agency – The Curriculum online.

www.dcsf.gov.uk/primarycurriculumreview/ Information relating to the Rose Report.

www.primaryreview.org.uk Information relating to the Cambridge Review.

7

Education for Social Justice

Chapter Outline

Introduction: Education as Social Justice

New Labour came to power in 1997 with the asserted belief that education and social justice are synonymous and it is useful to spend a few moments considering some different interpretations of what this might have meant. Classic definitions of social justice have often been divided into those emphasizing individual need and those focusing on the general good of the community (Artiles *et al.*, 2009). The individualistic model, as it suggests, promotes the redistribution of resources and the importance of providing equal access to the same curriculum, something that was central to the original National Curriculum of 1988. A variation on this model, which has come increasingly to the fore in government policy, is the 'libertarian' (Christensen and Dorn, 1997, cited in Artiles *et al.*, 2009). This locates the core of social justice as being dependent on individual merit being recognized and rewarded; a view which fits very well with the market forces approach to education in general, that is, an individual has the right to keep what they have earned.

Individualistic perspectives resonate with a worrying trend clearly seen in New Labour's policy, that is, 'Schools are increasingly based on an individual merit approach as educational achievement and failure are seen as the results of individuals' efforts and ability; as long as students have opportunity to compete, failure is therefore interpreted as an individual outcome' (Varenne and McDermott, 1999, cited in Artiles *et al.*, 2009, p. 46). As such, the state is cleared of responsibility as the onus for finding success through the education system is placed entirely on the shoulders of the individual student. Thus, structural problems in society remain unaddressed and the contextual and sociological issues relating to where a school might be situated, the economic circumstances of the parents or the rapid teacher turnover, for example, are totally ignored.

In contrast, a *communitarian social justice model* relies on the values of a community to create a cohesive and just society. According to Artiles *et al.*, 'From this perspective, social justice is achieved by maintaining responsibilities and rights in a symmetrical relationship' (2009, p. 46). Thus, communities are supposed to build alliances with others, whose values they share, in order to decide on common goals that influence educational opportunities. This model does not take into account those minority groups which do not feel represented by such values. There is also the possibility that the values of the most vocal group are not those of the majority, who remain relatively silent, and, therefore, more extreme factions can have their views taken into account in the spirit of inclusion.

Bull suggests that 'the principles of social justice in education are, in practice, hopelessly inconsistent with one another', and, moreover, that imposing common performance standards in an attempt to provide equal opportunities leads to 'the neglect of children's personal and political liberties' (2009, p. 147). Equal does not mean the same!

In concluding, Artiles *et al.* (2009, p. 51) offer some hope in the form of a *transformative model of social justice* which encourages participation by communities together with a fair distribution of resources as 'the foundation of democratic egalitarian alternatives'. In such a model, underlying social inequalities and their origins would be taken into account and meritocratic school systems would be challenged. Schools would act more as facilitators in the formulation of children's identities which would enable them 'to develop the differential abilities required for success' including economic capability (Bull, 2009, p. 144).

Social Justice in Education

As previously stated, shortly before gaining power in 1997, Tony Blair famously declared that education is synonymous with social justice, and, in some respects, there has been a genuine focus in Labour's policy on encouraging children from those groups which have been traditionally served less well by the education system to achieve greater success. However, as with the Conservatives before them, achievement has inevitably been measured in terms of quantitative data publishable in league tables, and as such, there has remained an emphasis on the individual child or student being able to find their way through the maze of potential routes in order to reach salvation. Therefore, Labour has held on to a reluctance to face up to more structural inequalities in society.

The strategies put in place by New Labour have continued to shy away from addressing issues such as how racism, classism and so on are deeply embedded in society and its institutions, and instead adopt a liberal approach of tweaking the edges of issues, providing catch-up initiatives and inevitably placing the onus on the 'victim'. So, for example, underachievement is often separated out from related issues such as the negative media representation of certain groups, or, indeed, poverty. Throughout, a central failure of successive government policies has been the lack of anti-racist education, for example.

As far back as 1988, the Education Reform Act had set the tone. It proposed to emphasize choice and diversity, and had introduced equal opportunities as a cross-curricular dimension which would 'permeate' the whole curriculum. However, as we have seen in Chapter 6, this was a nonassessed element of an already overcrowded curriculum and merely promoted cultural pluralism while strategies to combat racism more overtly remained inadequate. Teachers inevitably concentrated on the subjects which took centre stage and on whose results they would be judged. Eventually, Citizenship became the repository of hope with regard to where issues of social justice might be raised with pupils, but many schools failed to develop this fully and it remained a missed opportunity. Citizenship as a statutory subject, introduced in 2002, offered another chance to bring the equality agenda into the formal curriculum, but there was far too much content to be delivered successfully and the emphasis was more heavily weighted in favour of responsibilities rather than rights.

There has also been a possible reluctance on the part of teachers which Hassan (2009) refers to when she makes a perceptive comment that the 'assumed innocence of children' hinders 'an informed debate'. Too often, perhaps, it has been easier to hide behind the notion that children are unaware of the issues of inequality, and, for that reason, it would be heinous for teachers to destroy that innocence by focusing attention on such controversial topics in the classroom. Similar arguments are put forward when dealing with issues of sexual orientation. (For an accessible account of the historical perspective on social policies and race, see Hassan, 2009.) Consider your own experience of multicultural education and whether or not it is racism in disguise or indeed the acceptance of 'otherness' (Parekh, 2000).

The Nature of Prejudice

Allport (1979) explores the nature of prejudice as defined by the New English Dictionary as 'a feeling, favourable or unfavourable, towards a person or thing, prior to, or not based on actual experience', and he goes on to add that our dislike of whole groups of people can simply result from the fact that they are members of that group. However, interestingly, a prejudgement becomes a prejudice only when we cling stubbornly to our mistaken beliefs after being exposed to contrary evidence. In fact, we can even become emotional when our prejudices are threatened (ibid., p. 9).

When institutionalized, the sources of ethnic prejudice stem from false generalizations which involve 'cognitive, ego, emotional, cultural and personal factors' (ibid.). Allport also explains that sometimes it is easier for human beings to stay in groups where we feel comfortable and do not have to make great efforts to understand other cultures or language, for example. Of course, it is also true that members of minority groups may also prefer to stay within their own ethnic groups for the same reasons, yet the majority culture often finds this threatening.

The same may well be true when dealing with other groups with which we are less familiar. Ward and Eden (2009, p. 129) refer to the ways that a culture of 'laddish behaviour' is tolerated in the classroom rather than challenged as it is perhaps easier to remain with the status quo. Girls who adopt what teachers regard as male aggressive behaviour have become a threatening group for many teachers; the increasing numbers of exclusions for such girls are discussed elsewhere in this chapter. Ward and Eden also suggest that the culture and language of the classroom has yet to be fully analysed, particularly with reference to gender identity.

Educational Equality and the Law

Access and Opportunity

Technically, all British citizens have the right to be treated equally under the law; however, there are many interpretations of what this actually means and laws become reality when operationalized through people's behaviour. Inequality of access has often been seen as an obvious form of exclusion where irrelevant criteria become a barrier to certain groups being allowed 'into' an organization, resulting in injustice. Again, under the law, pupils have equal access to the same curriculum but it is still the case that some pupils are better placed to benefit from the education system than others. Gaine and George explore less overt examples of the ways in which exclusion can operate. They suggest that

> through the curriculum that is offered, the style of interaction in classrooms and the atmosphere in corridors – all aspects of schooling. . . . equality of opportunity, therefore, means opportunities without unfair barriers or irrelevant criteria getting in the way. It does not mean every pupil's results will be the same. (1999, pp. 3, 4)

Equality of outcome has always been the most problematic for teachers as the degree to which professionals can compensate for pupils' particular circumstances has remained a contentious subject. However, over the past few decades, numerous steps have been taken to attempt to remove unfair barriers throughout the population.

The first education act to frame the problem of inequality was the 1944 Education Act in which it was recognized that poverty was an issue as Britain was nearing the end of the Second World War. Ironically, we are now entering an era when poverty and class are becoming key factors in educational achievement once more, following decades when other aspects of social justice had become more dominant.

Gender Equality

It was a number of years before a combination of grassroots pressure and legal imperatives from Europe led to the introduction of the Sex Discrimination Act in 1975. The act had distinct sections relating to educational institutions and gave equal access to the curriculum for both boys and girls. It marked a recognition that teachers and schools had a role to play in equalizing society, but, according to Gaine and George (1999), the act was somewhat forced upon the British government. Subsequent acts extended the awareness of equality issues. The Equal Pay Act (1976) set the precedent of equal pay for work of equal value and women teachers were one of the groups who saw this as an opportunity to stake their claim to recognition of the value of their contribution to school life. Teachers are skilled at keeping detailed records and therefore at presenting successful tribunals challenging the position of many male heads of department, for example, in the fields of Design Technology and PE. In the same year, the Race Relations Act also became law and contained clauses making it unlawful for schools to discriminate against pupils of different ethnic backgrounds, either directly or indirectly, in matters of curriculum access, admissions, uniform, catering and so on.

In 1984, the Technical and Vocational Educational Initiative (TVEI) contained a commitment to equality of opportunity, which placed a demand on schools in receipt of funding to develop more robust policies and demonstrate a greater understanding of social justice through organizational and curriculum matters. Such initiatives as 'Girls into Science and Technology' (GIST) and 'Women into Science and Engineering' (WISE) focused on trying to reduce gender stereotyping with regard to subject and career choice, and were in many ways supported by the introduction of the National Curriculum in 1988 and its cross-curricular dimensions. For the first time, it became a legal requirement for schools to provide equal access for boys and girls to the same statutory curriculum. However, the favoured approach was always liberal, that is, a perspective that promoted amending the status quo rather than seriously challenging it in far more radical ways. Thus, the sexist nature of gendered subject choice remained through such influences as teachers' and employers' own prejudices, peer pressure and organizational pragmatism. In recent years, of course, the focus of teachers' attentions has shifted to the underachievement of boys.

Race Equality

In terms of race, Gaine and George (1999) acknowledge the unusual relationship that has existed for centuries between the education system and religion, a relationship which is markedly absent in other countries such as France, despite their more overt religious observance. The Education Reform Act of 1988, in fact, moved schools firmly back to a curriculum which placed Christianity at its centre, much to the dismay of many teachers who had welcomed the gradual shift towards a humanistic daily meeting for pupils, reflecting the multiethnic composition of the pupil body. Previously, educational approaches to pupils from different cultural backgrounds had moved through distinct phases. The 1960s had marked a period of assimilation, with the emphasis firmly on enabling 'newcomers' to acquire fluent English language, and other community languages were definitely seen as inferior and to be discouraged.

Liberal Traditions

During the 1970s educational institutions were encouraged to adopt a multicultural approach to the curriculum (Gaine and George, 1999) which was as liberal as the equal opportunities approach to gender issues. Ward and Eden observe that 'multicultural education gained a strong foothold in the consciousness of teachers and local authority officers' (2009, p. 138), and go on to describe teachers who promoted such teaching strategies as 'informed professionals'. Multicultural education, however, was mainly developed in those areas of the country that appeared to be most diverse in terms of their population, such as London, Manchester, Leicester and Birmingham and which were, moreover, under Labour-controlled authorities. It was largely ignored in rural areas and, in fact, was frequently limited to subject areas that were perceived to be less important or to tokenistic events and celebratory days. As such, 'strangeness' and notions of difference were often reinforced.

Radical Approaches

A more radical attack on curriculum bias developed in the 1980s, known as anti-racist education ,which resulted in some teachers choosing to encourage classroom debate where notions of power could be explored and school hierarchies challenged. During the early 1980s the UK suffered from a series of uprisings in inner-city areas where communities turned on themselves. This was a shocking occurrence for the government which ordered an investigation by Lord Rampton. The subsequent Swann Report, published in 1985, was considerably softened in its findings but did recommend that teachers should include a multicultural perspective on the curriculum wherever they taught in the UK, in Devon and Clwyd as much as in inner cities (the notion that any discrimination on the part of professionals is 'unintentional' was a message to be repeated in the 1999 McPherson Report many years later, following the death of Stephen Lawrence). Anti-racism was soundly ignored in the legislation that followed, namely, the 1988 Act, although committed teachers and advisers placed their faith in the existence of the cross-curricular dimension and the introduction of Citizenship (see Chapter 6) through which they could continue to promote the equality cause.

Multiculturalism and Social Justice

Patel presents an interesting argument regarding the acceptance of multiculturalism which had developed in the UK at least as far as government policy was concerned, despite there being 'a long-standing concern' on the part of some educators. However, after the bombing in London, Patel (2007) claims that this attitude changed, and Ward and Eden agree that Labour became less committed to eradicating racism, allowing religion to become 'the centre of the debate' (2009, p. 144). Is it possible, as Patel suggests, that anti-racist, secular education is now facing a challenge from 'the increasing assertion of religion as the main badge of identity'? (2007, p. 262).

As we considered at the start of this chapter, the willingness to see social justice as a political force for structural change has somewhat weakened, and emphasis has shifted towards a respect for cultural difference often related to religion. This has been absorbed into an inclusion agenda in many schools and was indicative of New Labour's policy of marketization and diversity (Ward and Eden, 2009). According to Patel, there are two emerging trends: first, anti-racist and multicultural approaches to education are both being subsumed into 'multi-faithism'; and second, this focus on religion is having an effect on black and minority ethnic girls who sometimes find themselves forced into a more traditional mode of behaviour by extremist faith groups exerting pressure on schools. Moreover, Patel's research points to an interesting phenomenon, that is, teachers have come to ascribe religious issues to pupils from South Asian origin while more overt political resistance is seen as being a characteristic of Afro-Caribbean behaviour. In addition, conflicts of interest between issues of gender and religion are more likely to be ignored. The effect on teachers can be an unwillingness to challenge sensitive issues or attitudes for fear of falling foul of religious sensibilities.

If, as Patel (2007) maintains, references to Asian culture are usually confined to religious festivals and practices, does this serve to allow religious extremists to find their way into the school curriculum? If headteachers are fearful of being branded racists or against equal opportunities, does this make them more likely to be responsive to the demands of parent groups, however small? Of course, this scenario would also include the voices of Christian fundamentalist groups. Such an argument would help to explain why some, not all, Muslim parents see the advantages of single-sex schooling as an aid in their battle to limit the participation of young women in society in general. Patel's case study (2007) contains the experiences of some headteachers and the decisions they have to grapple with in this regard.

One further consequence of government policy prioritizing inclusion in relation to faith is the growing number of parents who request the withdrawal of their children from certain areas of the school curriculum. Sex and Relationship Education is an obvious source of conflict (Patel, 2007) while Religious Education is another. It is interesting to ask the question regarding which groups are expected to be inclusive in their approach to the curriculum and which are allowed to be exclusive in the name of inclusion? The acceptance of the rights of pupils and teachers who are lesbian, gay, bi-sexual or transgender is problematic for a number of other oppressed groups, and it remains to be seen how faith groups will respond to the new guidance on domestic violence education being introduced to schools. The logical end of the continuum would result in a greater number of parents opting out of state education altogether; but in the meantime, teachers are left trying to balance the growing rights of parents with the rights of their children to a democratic and socially just education. As Ward and Eden (2009) argue, if community schools were more inclusive, then there would be fewer demands for separate/faith-based schools. As Patel states:

> The school context provides the most conducive environment in which to nurture individual minds. It is about the potential to contribute to the construction of a unifying identity based on notions of social justice, equality and human rights. But in the current climate, state schools appear to be

contributing to an agenda which promotes a new settlement between religion and the state in which religion is beginning to occupy a more prominent and privileged public role. At the very least, this development indicates the threat of further segregation, intolerance and inequality based around religious divisions. (2007, pp. 273–4)

Consider:

- Race: Black History Month in October. Was it celebrated in your school or college? What events took place? Was there a focus on African-Caribbean history?
- Religion: Should religion be kept out of state schools entirely? If you attended a religious school, what do you consider were the benefits of the education you experienced there?

Recent Legislation

The first part of the Disability Discrimination Act was passed in 1995, the impact of which was not on the curriculum at all but instead placed a duty upon educational institutions to consider employing people with disabilities as having the same rights as able-bodied candidates. There was still no government interference to ensure that recommended quotas of people from underrepresented groups were, in fact, being adopted; however, it added fuel to the arguments of those parents who wished to see their children accepted into mainstream educational institutions.

Following Labour's election victory in 1997, there 'has been an unprecedented number of laws designed to achieve equality and combat . . . discrimination' (McIntyre, 2009, p. 301). Significant among them was the Race Relations (Amendment) Act of 2000 which was eventually passed as an outcome of the murder of the black teenager, Stephen Lawrence. This brought into being a new era for all public bodies, including schools and education authorities, demanding that all aspects of institutional life were to be scrutinized in order to ensure the promotion of active policies on equality. It acknowledged the existence of 'institutional racism' for the first time and called for schools, among others, to draw up policies governing all aspects of school life, as well as keeping detailed monitoring data including the logging of racist incidents and bullying.

The Human Rights Act, 2000, also had implications for schools; for example, it banned any humiliating punishments being used against pupils and protected their privacy in the case of searching bags and so on. Further legislation relating to disability access was passed in 2002, known as SENDA, which had implications for pupils who wanted to attend mainstream schools, as well as establishing the need to adapt the physical design of all public amenities.

With regard to sexuality, a number of laws have been introduced since 2000 which aim to provide greater protection for those who are LGBT (lesbian, gay, bisexual or transgendered).

These include the repeal of Section 28 which had either frightened teachers into avoiding mentioning sexuality issues for fear of being accused of promoting sexuality, or been used as an excuse by those who had no wish to confront such issues in schools. There is also the Sexual Offences Bill (2000) relating to the age of consent, the Equality Act (Sexual Orientation Regulations) of 2007 and Stand Up for Us: challenging homophobia in schools (2004).

More recently, all aspects of social justice have been addressed at least in name, with such additions to the Equality Act as Age (2006), Religion or Belief (2003) and the Gender Equality Duty (2007). Most of these have placed duties on schools to provide policies demonstrating how they promote equality across all aspects of school life, including against bullying. These are expected to be accompanied by action plans to explain how the policies are being implemented, and detailed guidance is available for specific areas of the public sector. We are now at a stage where organizations are carrying out impact assessments in all areas and these have certainly been taken seriously by universities and colleges.

Currently, a single equalities commission has been established with a new bill, passed in April 2010, which came into force in October. This will be monitored by the Equality and Human Rights Commission (EHRC) which has published six pieces of draft guidance on employment, services and related areas and also education. From 2010, there will be a single public sector equality duty including a greater emphasis on discrimination by association and perception; therefore, how pupils perceive themselves being treated will have more weight in any procedure. Of course, this will also work for teachers who feel they have been treated unfavourably.

Labour's comprehensive delivery plan for the year leading up to the introduction of the new Equality Act included priorities for every area of policy relating to equality of opportunity. The detail was as specific as increasing the uptake of school lunches; closing the attainment gap in the foundation stage between children from disadvantaged groups and others; reducing the exclusion rates for those with special needs (acknowledging that this is an important factor); considering ways to reduce the gender pay gap and involving children and young people more actively in policy development. Many of these were not fulfilled by the time that Labour lost power in the election in May 2010.

Interestingly, equality could prove to be a source of division between the coalition parties in future. We are unlikely to return to the outright opposition to strategies relating to equality and social justice that we witnessed under the government of Margaret Thatcher, but according to the new Chief Executive of the Universities' Equalities Challenge Unit, we are unlikely to see the same level of interest in the next few years that has characterized the last 13.

Responses to Equal Opportunities Legislation

One inevitable response to the number and detail of equality legislation and guidance for public bodies was the criticism from right-wing media that things had gone too far and political correctness had completely taken over. This was epitomized by the diatribe against teachers' unions which supported a case of racist bullying in a school that eventually involved the police (Richardson, 2006). The school was perceived to have not responded appropriately to the incident, and after a prolonged period of name calling followed by physical attack, the parents went to the police. What is interesting here according to Richardson is the reaction from certain newspapers who branded the leaders of major teachers' unions as 'hags and thought police' (2006, p. 183) for publicly acknowledging that there were serious issues involved for which there was detailed government guidance available. It is also an example of two opposing professional reactions to policy on equality, one upholding legal government initiatives as necessary and indeed 'central and foundational in the education enterprise' (Richardson, 2006, p. 186), the other claiming that teachers themselves were guilty of invoking yet another moral panic by ascribing too much importance to children's aggression based on racist attitudes.

Another manifestation of the way in which schools have failed to fully incorporate recent government policy has been the ongoing differential rates of exclusions for pupils from particular backgrounds. 'Black and Caribbean pupils are just over three times as likely as White pupils to be permanently excluded from school' (Parsons *et al.*, 2005, p. 1) and this is in a context where permanent exclusions generally have continued to fall. Other groups who are most likely to be excluded are Irish Travellers, Gypsy/Roma, Mixed Heritage pupils and, according to Carlile (2009), working-class girls. In the primary sector, exclusions seem to be more common among children with Special Education Needs while Black pupils continue to be excluded from special schools in greater numbers than other groups.

The Race Relations Amendment Act and Gender Equality Acts have placed clear duties on schools to assess the impacts of their policies and practices on particular vulnerable groups and to establish an action plan to deal with any obvious injustices. However, Parsons *et al.* (2005) maintain that many schools are not yet complying fully with the spirit of the law. School policies with respect to equality have come under the remit of Ofsted inspectors and there has been nationwide training on how to implement the laws correctly, but there are many policies which are not accompanied by action plans or impact assessments. Inspectors have praised some schools for their accepting ethos, their collection of data and the establishment of a range of mentoring schemes, as well as their attempts to create better links with parents and use of restorative justice; however, Parsons *et al.* (2005) observe that inspection reports do not interpret the statistics that demonstrate the disproportionate exclusions of groups covered by the legislation. Carlile goes so far as to interpret the pattern of permanent exclusions of girls as institutionalized sexism (2009, p. 333) and comments on teachers' construction of young Black females as 'marginalized' and troublesome 'others' (Wright, 2004, cited in Carlile, 2009). Working-class girls' behaviour is often seen by teachers as overly aggressive and, moreover, oversexualized. Descriptions used during exclusion panel discussions frequently focus on the pupils' physical size and become what Carlile calls 'gendered narratives' (2009, p. 334).

Carlile concludes that 'some permanent exclusions from school happen because of habitual assumptions about pupils and their families and a lack of knowledge of the grinding chronic inequities they can suffer' (2009, p. 342). It is not deliberate on teachers' part, Carlile acknowledges, but relates to the point made earlier that it is sometimes easier to retreat into the familiar. Another interesting argument is that such strategies as exclusion are also inevitable in light of the fatigue felt by many teachers who are worn down by the many relentless pressures the teaching profession has faced from successive governments.

Schools which were most successful at reducing the number of such exclusions were those where senior staff and governors understood the implications of the acts and had also made good use of funding available through such initiatives as Excellence in Cities, Behaviour Improvement Programmes and so on. Others have demonstrated a willingness to compromise on issues such as uniform where it is possible; for example, to allow girls to wear a long version of the school skirt in order to accommodate the preferences of Muslim pupils. This sends a message of welcome and an acceptance of diversity which, in turn, helps to reduce the likelihood of excluding on the grounds of 'difference'.

Moral Panics and Policy Hysteria

The area of social justice has often been one that attracts a certain amount of hysteria which can be described as a form of 'moral panic'. The moral panic is a scare about a threat or supposed threat from deviants or 'folk-devils'; a category of people who, presumably, engage in evil practices and are blamed for menacing a society's culture, way of life and central values. The word 'scare' implies that the 'fear of or hostility towards the folk-devil is out of proportion to the actual threat that is claimed' (Goode and Ben-Yehuda, 2009, p. 2).

Characteristics of such scares include the fact that the scare is out of all proportion to any real or perceived threat, and often claims are exaggerated or, indeed, nonexistent. The 'objects' of the scare are often demonized and the overexaggerated response can be further heightened by media coverage. The issue, however, has to capture the public imagination or it will remain a concern of reporters alone. There are certain phenomena which are necessary for a moral panic to develop and theories relating to this can be divided into three types:

- Marxists tend to see such phenomena as being 'engineered' by the 'elite' who 'fabricate, orchestrate or engineer a panic from a non-existent or trivial threat . . . to divert attention away from issues that threaten their own interests' (Goode and Ben-Yehuda, 2009, p. 54).
- Interest group theorists see moral panics as coming from influential middle groups such as journalists or professionals.
- The grassroots model suggests that 'fears' spring up naturally out of concerns shared by relatively large numbers of people.

Two further requirements are necessary for a moral panic to truly occur and these are the existence of the target group or 'folk devil' or a disaster mentality. Interestingly, with regard to social justice, Goode and Ben-Yehuda suggest that 'moral panics are likely to demonstrate that there are limits to how much diversity can be tolerated in a society' (2009, p. 29). Thus such occurrences help to divide society into 'us' and 'them'.

Panics usually involve concern and anxiety about the preservation of certain values or traditions and hostility towards the target or 'out' group. There is fairly widespread agreement that there is a threat which is often exaggerated out of all proportion. Such phenomena can erupt suddenly, arising out of facts that have been distorted or even 'invented' and can disappear equally quickly. They thrive on rumour. An obvious example of this is the fall-out after 9/11 which schools with multiethnic intake have frequently found challenging. Reactions can include the introduction of control measures, often implemented by the police. Politicians can be quick to seize the opportunity to impress their public by swift and dramatic legal responses, but the answers are not necessarily obvious and can lead to a great deal of debate.

Issues relating to education that have developed characteristics of moral panics include:

- Islamophobia
- failing boys
- underachievement
- failure of minority ethnic groups
- failing schools
- antisocial behaviour among young people
- the over-riding concern around 'standards'.

Ward and Eden point out that the attention given to boys' underachievement has led teachers to focus on keeping the boys occupied in class, while government approaches have contained the implicit message that 'the problem of the achievement gap can be solved within the school system' (2009, p. 125). The teacher has been blamed to an extent for the phenomenon of boys' relative failure, and underachievement has become one of the government's greatest obsessions. The reasons for boys' disillusionment with the education system are many and complex. The demands of the academic curriculum are just one of the components alongside the changing nature of employment in the Western world, peer pressure, the complex behaviour of the classroom and ongoing gendered preferences with regard to assessment and curriculum content. There is also the consideration that teachers have always struggled with working-class boys' behaviour; there never really was a golden age when all children obeyed rules without question. The issue has become acute in the light of recent obsessions with achievement, which is seen in terms of performance data only. Government has responded by introducing a plethora of initiatives aimed at countering the consequences of underachievement, for example, criminal behaviour and social exclusion; thus initiatives such as mentoring schemes, homework clubs, extended schools and breakfast clubs have flourished, often funded through Excellence in Cities, Behaviour Improvement Programmes and Education Action Zones. Many of these schemes have provided valuable experiences for children, but behind them all lay the anxieties about Britain's economic performance and competitiveness which are increasingly related to school performance. The UK is not alone in this respect.

A recent chapter in the history of moral panics in education has been documented by McIntyre (2009) in her research on teachers' attitudes towards lesbian, gay and bi-sexual pupils in secondary schools in Scotland. McIntyre actually defines her second major finding as 'Moral panic. No sex please we're teachers' (ibid., p. 305). Here she discusses the complex contradictions of schools as sites where children must be protected from their own developing sexual awareness and where teachers see themselves as the protector. Notions of children as 'sexualized beings' were regarded as completely at odds with society's expectations of schools as desexualized places. McIntyre (2009) refers to a major study by Epstein and Johnson (1998) emphasizing the fact that teachers frequently felt anxiety when any discussion of sexuality occurred, with male primary teachers being the most affected. Ironically, children are exposed to a greater variation of role models through the media, some of whom, it is true, might be considered inappropriate, and it is well documented that even young children can express gendered behaviour, frequently stereotypically. However, teachers' anxiety and confusion over how best to deal with such matters is understandable in today's society.

Teachers in the context of present-day schooling are under increasing scrutiny and experience a high level of accountability. Wrigley refers to these changes in education as 'full spectrum surveillance' (2006, cited in McIntyre, 2009, p. 305). McIntyre goes on to suggest that teachers are perceived as less trustworthy professionals than they used to be and it is certainly true that trainee teachers are given detailed advice about protecting themselves before embarking on any school placement. McIntyre also puts forward the interesting notion that when children deviate from the apparent 'norm' of heterosexuality, this causes a moral panic for teachers. Indeed, they seem to interpret their 'duty of care' as taking it upon themselves to try and influence a child away from becoming anything other than heterosexual. Far from challenging homophobia, schools often retreat into a celebration of male macho culture, using humour as a refuge, complete silence or both, and refusal to discuss the existence of anything other than heterosexuality out of fear that society itself may be under threat. The next section provides a more detailed focus on how schools and teachers deal with the issue of sexual identity.

Focus on: Schools and homophobia

An important issue for schools today is how they can incorporate strategies for promoting diversity and inclusion 'in their day to day lives' (Warwick et al., 2004, p. 1). This becomes even more complex when there are a number of reports describing the impact of homophobic bullying within educational

Focus on: Schools and homophobia (cont'd)

institutions. The culture that develops from ignoring discrimination and different forms of bullying can have harmful effects on both students and staff. Warwick *et al.* go on to state that 'homophobia by pupils and staff can contribute to teacher stress, lack of confidence, poor work achievements, resignations and being overlooked for promotions' (2004, p. 1). A shocking statistic shows that in secondary schools in England and Wales, around 82 per cent of teachers are aware that verbal homophobic bullying is happening and 26 per cent are even aware of physical attacks (ibid.). McIntyre supports this view, agreeing that 'homophobic bullying is common in schools but often ignored by teachers and there is an assumption that all pupils are heterosexual' (2009, p. 302). Moreover, while 'government policy and guidance tends to take an anti-homophobia and more explicitly, anti-bullying stance,' DePalma and Atkinson maintain that this is not enough to prevent stereotyping and heterosexist assumptions and call for teachers to 'reach beyond passive and disingenuous tolerance . . . to proactively incorporate discussions of sexuality and gender into their curriculum' (2009, p. 838). They acknowledge that many of the teachers' stories 'sustained fears, motivations and silences' (ibid., p. 841), yet such silences allow the continued oppression of children and young people with the inevitable results.

Reported incidents have led to suicide, truancy, underachievement and a desire to leave education as soon as possible. This is all despite the evidence that young people are now seeing more positive images of a spectrum of sexual identities in society in general, but as McIntyre (2009, p. 301) asserts, 'this acceptance has been slower to transfer to the institution of the family and the school.' McIntyre references a number of research studies to support her argument that neither teacher trainers nor trainees consider sexuality issues relevant to pedagogy. She summarizes their findings as identifying 'how mention of both LGBT pupils and issues surrounding them are missing in the taught and hidden curriculum' (ibid.). This is reminiscent of the barriers faced by Black and Minority Ethnic pupils and teachers in previous decades, which is in effect, the problem of invisibility. However, McIntyre suggests several notions to help explain teachers' sensitivity which perhaps relate more particularly to sexual identity:

- Schools are very much public places whereas sexuality is regarded very much as a personal matter (Epstein and Johnson, 1998, cited in McIntyre, 2009).
- It is possible that teachers are disinclined to see children as 'sexualized beings', particularly in light of recent legislation and strict safeguarding initiatives under the banner of child protection.

Research by McIntyre (2009) leads her to the conclusion that teachers do not have the language to discuss the diversity of sexuality. Instead, many teachers and school policies have reverted to the safety of pretending that in their professional capacities, they do not perceive difference in any way 'that the normative is natural rather than socially constructed' (DePalma and Atkinson, 2009, p. 841). 'In adopting a liberal approach of equality for all, they have interpreted equality to mean sameness' when it actually means 'respecting difference' (McIntyre, 2009, p. 309).

Nixon turns the situation on its head by suggesting that schools should employ LGBT teachers as valuable role models:

> . . . they force schools and other educational establishments to face reality in terms of continuing discrimination on the grounds of gender and sexuality, both within and without, and to begin the long, hard-fought process of setting up new models for thinking and behaviour. (2006, p. 280)

> ## Consider:
>
> - Is it possible to reconcile policies aimed at protecting children within schools with current legal demands to promote all forms of equality including sexuality?
> - Do you share some teachers' discomfort about acknowledging the range of sexual identities present in any school, classroom or staffroom?
> - Why is it important to have a curriculum that reflects all pupils' backgrounds?

Successful Practice

Whatever the form of social justice being considered, schools can use a combination of teaching activities focused around the issues, together with whole school strategies and policies to communicate the message that all pupils are equally deserving of respect and that discrimination will not be tolerated. Similarly, a positive school ethos, the support of colleagues and a general commitment to equality and diversity all create an environment where children know they are valued, whatever their personal circumstances. Teachers also need to have opportunities to discuss, explore and challenge their own attitudes and develop their knowledge of the groups which still receive an unequal experience of the education system simply because of who they are. Schools and teachers can play a vital role in providing places of safety for young people to explore their identities by sometimes having the courage 'to engage in professionally risky, ground-breaking equalities work' (DePalma and Atkinson, 2009, p. 845). However, as with all initiatives, the attitudes of senior leaders are vital for the success of any policy whether they be in the school itself, the local authority or, indeed, the government.

The Current Situation

The Resurgence of Class

In the recent, but now ignored, Cambridge Review of primary education, Robin Alexander suggested that child poverty remains one of the education system's greatest challenges (2008, p. 3). He also acknowledged that SATs results, however we may disagree with the method of testing, correlate closely with forms of inequality; in wealth, health, social mobility risk and opportunity (ibid.). Furthermore, children from the lowest socioeconomic groups in society are those who achieve the poorest grades: White, working-class boys, looked after children, children with disabilities and children from particular ethnic minority backgrounds including Travellers and refugees (ibid.).

Can these correlations be dismissed as a result of low parental aspirations? Is it more to do with school culture and the failure of providers to understand and respect diversity of family values, structures and practices? In fact, Alexander concludes that 'schools may provide the security, sense of purpose, positive values and sense of community which may be in decline outside the school gates'; and that in this capacity they have an increasingly important role to play in the promotion of social justice in an age of frightening economic uncertainty (2008, p. 6).

Factors Affecting Attainment

The different factors affecting White pupils' attainment, including those who have free school meals and those who do not, are largely related to parental income, employment, material status and interest in their children's education. Their prior attainment also contributes to their success or otherwise at KS 4. Interestingly, there is very little part played by school effectiveness and pupil aspirations. Therefore, we may conclude that social factors outside school have more impact on pupils' outcomes.

One interesting characteristic affecting attainment of minority ethnic groups is the factor of whether they are entitled to free school meals. However, pupils' aspirations are less significant although these may be higher than those of their White counterparts. Here schools do have a greater role to play in reducing the attainment gap. It is also interesting to note that pupils on free school meals are more likely to have special educational needs.

Barriers to Participation in Education and Training

For those young people who are outside education and training (NEETS) or in a low-skilled job where they do not receive any training, the cost of transport to and from work becomes a huge barrier. In fact, these groups, together with teenage parents, find finance a major problem when pursuing meaningful employment or training post-16. Some of these young people have to pay rent to their parents, and, not surprisingly, the more acute problems are faced by young people from the poorest backgrounds whose parents, themselves, are poorly qualified.

There is obviously a need for better information and financial support to be provided for the more vulnerable groups such as the NEETS, teenage parents and those from low-income families if they are to survive in an increasingly competitive working environment. This is another example of the resurgence of poverty and class as highly influential factors in children's success within education and beyond (see Spielhoffer et al., 2010).

Summary

Looking Back

From the outset, there has been a major contradiction at the heart of Labour policy between the pronouncements from Tony Blair in 1997 that social justice and education were synonymous and the obsession with performance tables and standards agenda defended by Estelle Morris 8 weeks after the election. Dyson (2009) argues that New Labour policies were genuinely designed to improve the economic performance of the country as a whole while improving the life chances of poorer people. Indeed, reforming the school system has been one way of trying to advance social justice that has been adopted by many Western governments taking similar approaches. These include increased central control of content and methodology in order to 'improve' schools; increasingly centralized assessment; and a focus on professional accountability and setting up 'quasi-markets' (Dyson, 2009, p. 39). Yet, a relentless programme of school educational reform has not narrowed the gap in educational achievements or in life chances between children from more and less disadvantaged backgrounds. Dyson (2009) refers to a number of studies (e.g. Hansen and Joshi, 2007; Cassen *et al.*, 2007) which indicate that social mobility has if anything declined. Dyson goes on to reaffirm that changing schools and funding initiatives may have their place, but that, in themselves, they cannot bring about social equality; while Varenne and McDermott (1999, cited in Artiles *et al.*, 2009, p. 46) observed that under New Labour, schools became increasingly based on a meritocracy where failure and achievement are both interpreted as the result of individual effort.

Brandsma (2002, p. 2) agrees that initiatives such as Educational Priority Areas were not a success in a number of countries, while unequal opportunities in education in general remain a persistent and evolving problem and complex prescriptive regulations do not necessarily produce guaranteed outcomes. Marketization of education has frequently led to greater disadvantage for those likely to face educational and social exclusion while the poor and least qualified are inevitably affected most by economic change. Brandsma (2002) also calls for compulsory education systems to find a way of reconciling the competing demands of promoting equality while increasing efficiency and maintaining high standards.

Looking Forward

In order to bring about a more just world in the future, Serf suggests that a global perspective to the curriculum is essential and calls for education to move from the transmissive to the transformative (2008, p. 414). He argues that students need to develop a sense of responsibility to others socially and globally in order to enjoy and value diversity, but that this can only be achieved if learners have a positive sense of personal identity and are confident in their own social and cultural context . . . are able to express their views and be aware of their own value systems (ibid.). Dyson (2009, p. 39) suggests refocusing on community schools which positively affect the community surrounding them, therefore impacting on social justice by area. Such strategies have already proved successful in the United States, for example, and Extended Schools in the UK have possibly provided a starting point. Brandsma calls for education and training institutions to open up and network with labour organizations and sociocultural institutions in order to enable the development of a more evolutionary approach to inequality and social exclusion in education and training (2002, p. 7). Similarly, Bull puts forward a 'dramatically different system of accountability . . . one in which central political authorities have a responsibility to hold localities accountable for the social justice purposes of education and in which local authorities have a responsibility to design the school curriculum to be genuinely responsive to the diverse cultural interests that children have in their local communities' (2009, p. 141).

The new Coalition government has quickly announced plans for schools to diversify even more dramatically than under New Labour, allowing groups of parents and others to establish their own so-called free schools that define new models of governance. Will these build on the ideas outlined above, and present us with a new and exciting model of community social justice, or will they focus more on segregation and keeping people out? Much will depend on teachers taking back responsibility for ensuring that social justice issues remain high on the agenda, an aspect inextricably linked to the re-professionalism of teachers. Key to this is the need for a renewed commitment from teacher trainers to foster understanding of the centrality of equality in the education system. We can only wait and hope.

Useful References

Goode, E. and Ben-Yehuda, N. (2009), *Moral Panics and the Social Construction of Deviance,* 2nd edn. Oxford: Wiley-Blackwell.

Sharp, J., Ward, S. and Hankin, L. (eds.) (2009), *Education Studies: An Issues-based Approach,* 2nd edn. Exeter: Learning Matters.

Ward, S. and Eden, C. (2009), *Key Issues in Education Policy.* London: Sage.

Useful Websites

www.ecu.ac.uk The Equality Challenge Unit.

www.equalityhumanrights.com The Equality and Human Rights Commission.

www.stonewall.org.uk *Stonewall* works for equality and justice for lesbians, gay men and bisexuals.

Teachers

Introduction

The 1950s were considered to have represented a 'golden era' for teachers and for teacher professionalism. At this time, teachers were viewed as 'partners [with the state] in the deliberations of policy, able to influence the direction and control of the system (Lawn, 1999 cited in Gillard, 2005, p. 176). Teachers were free to decide what to teach and how to teach it. Parents, too, trusted teachers to know what was best for their child. By the late 1970s, however, that golden era was over. Economic recession fuelled concerns about the failure of the education system. Teachers and their adoption of so-called progressive teaching methods were held responsible for the failings of the system. This complete disenchantment with the education system led to the then Prime Minister James Callaghan calling for a 'Great Debate' into the nature and purposes of education. Callaghan's agenda to reform education was, however, never realized. A General Election returned a Conservative Government which quickly set about 'putting teachers in their place' and instigating an 'era of name and shame' (Gillard, 2005, p. 177) in which teachers were no longer partners with the state but became its servants. As Ball highlights:

> Conservative neoliberals saw [teachers] as dangerously self-interested, a producer lobby resistant to change and risk averse, while for neoconservatives they were dangerously radical and progressive, responsible for too much change and politically motivates, not to be trusted . . . Such 'blaming' was tied to a supposed 'lack of accountability' and provided the legitimation for greater oversight, control of and intervention into teachers' work. (2008, pp. 143–4)

Throughout the Conservative years the teaching profession was held in derision and, as we will see, under New Labour, teachers have only fared slightly better, with policies continuing to 'undermine teacher morale and status' (Gillard, 2005). As a result, as Ball points out, 'Inside classrooms teachers are [now] caught between the imperatives of prescription and the disciplines of performance. Their practice is both "steered" and "rowed". It is still the case that teachers are not trusted' (2008, p. 150). The policy packages that New Labour in particular have used to reform the teaching profession – professional standards, performance management, target setting and professional development have been formed into a sort of 'governmental project' that has 'sought to render teachers increasingly subservient to the state and the agencies of the state' (Beck, 2008, p. 119 cited in Storey, 2009, p. 2).

Teacher Professionalism – Changing Identities

Professionalism

'How should we understand the role of the teacher?' (Whitty, 2006b, p. 1) and how appropriate are existing notions of teacher professionalism in the current context. Professionalism is not an easy concept to define and has more recently become a word that is 'synonymous with occupation' (Morrell, 2003, p. 1). Indeed, the word is often used these days to mean doing your job well, whatever kind of job that may be. Pickard and Powell define professionalism as:

> the possession and exercise of exclusive skills related to a body of knowledge onerously acquired and, in the public sector at least, an altruistic attitude towards those who are the object of professional attention. (2005, p. 2)

However, they also admit that this is possibly a benign and over-simplified definition. Professionalism is not considered in contemporary literature to be a fixed category, but is one that changes and shifts according to the social and political context (Ozga, 2009).

According to Leaton Gray (2006, p. 309) evidence from the literature suggests the following characteristics of a profession:

- The possession of an exclusive body of knowledge
- The ability to determine own fees
- Autonomy with respect to working practices
- Self regulation by members of the profession
- Promotion of members interests within society
- Guaranteed integrity, standards and ethical codes of practice
- Altruism.

When defining what constitutes a professional role, therefore, we often include such notions as having undergone theoretical training, having a dedication to service and possessing a degree of autonomy (Morrell, 2003). This privilege is often accompanied by the acceptance of working long hours, going beyond the 'norm' and having a special agreement and trust between the professional and the 'clients'.

Whitty (2006b) acknowledges that recent views on teacher professionalism have become less fixed while noting the growing feminist critique of a concept of professionalism that is exclusive and patriarchal. Some teachers, themselves, dislike the term as being essentially elitist. However, over the past decade, the government's own model of professionalism has come to dominate the agenda by demanding certain forms of behaviour in return for salaries. Whitty (2006b citing Sachs, 2003) defines the modern professional as one who does as s/he is told efficiently while being fully accountable for their actions.

Leaton Gray suggests that 'teaching is not necessarily a profession in the traditional sense of the word' (2006, p. 310). While some aspects of teachers' working practices can be viewed as professional, other aspects, such as, for example, the fact that teachers do not determine their own pay nor do they have autonomy over their working practices, together with the lack of trust invested in them, actually deny them true professional status. In fact, teachers have never been able to exercise the degree of professional autonomy to regulate their own affairs that other professions like medicine and the law have enjoyed (Whitty, 2006b). As one of the largest teaching unions, the Association of Teachers and Lecturers (2008), comment 'professionals use their skills and knowledge to exercise judgement in dealing with their clients [however, recently] important judgements about curriculum, assessment and pedagogy have been removed from teachers' and as a consequence teachers now merely implement decisions made elsewhere.

Notions of teacher professionalism are actually many and varied. According to the ATL, 'teaching is an *intellectual profession,* based on a high degree of general and systemised knowledge' (2008, p. 1); however, they also acknowledge that teaching is also practical, and has a wide range of practices and methods while also having a basis in care and responsibility. As a consequence, as professionals, teachers have to be highly adaptable. Hargreaves (1998 cited in Hill, 2007, p. 7) refers to teaching as 'emotional practice' which needs 'emotional understanding,' while Mahony and Hextall insist that 'teaching involves relationships between people whose persona, social, economic, cultural and political identities and positionings are complex' and that to manage such relationships requires 'sophisticated professional skills' (1997, p. 152). The awareness that, as professionals, teachers have to reconcile their own values with those of the institutions in which they work, could be key to understanding some of the tensions within the teaching profession. Those who try to hold on to old ideas of what it means to be a good teacher have sometimes had difficulty in embracing 'the new managerial role expected of them' (Hill, 2007, p. 17).

As previously observed, teaching has never enjoyed the status of the more 'elite' professions such as medicine and the law and is often described as a 'quasi-profession' (Whitty, 2006b, p. 3). It is, however, interesting to note that even doctors were forced into a new professional contract 'devised by a grocer's daughter and advised by the chief executive of Sainsbury's' (Morrell, 2003, p. 2) as a result of Margaret Thatcher's deep suspicion of professionalism in general. Hill (2007) also presents the possibility that an hierarchical interpretation of the low status of the teaching profession could be related to the number of women employed in education; as an historically female profession, teaching does not receive the respect accorded to fields that are more masculine. Freedman *et al.* (2008, p. 13) highlight four main reasons for the relatively low status of the teaching profession as identified by Purvis in 1973:

- Teaching is perceived as a less glamorous job than either medicine or the law
- People's sustained contact with teachers, as a consequence of their own schooling, means that the role is familiar and therefore has less mystique attached to it than say that of a doctor
- Teachers tend to have lower qualifications than members of other professions
- Teaching is often viewed as something 'anyone can do' and teachers as having slipped into teaching because they could not find anything else to do.

Barber (2005, cited in Whitty, 2006b, p. 2; see also Dainton, 2005, p. 161) presents an often contested narrative of four distinct phases with regard to the development of teachers' professional status:

- *Uninformed Professionalism.* Up to the 1980s (alternatively seen as the golden age of teacher autonomy)
- *Uninformed Prescription.* During the Thatcher years leading up to the National curriculum (compliance)
- *Informed Prescription.* Under New Labour where we see the beginnings of 'evidence based' policies and the introduction of standards for teacher training
- *Informed Professionalism.* From 2005 to the present where, having decided that teachers were to be trusted again, they are once more be granted a degree of freedom.

Whitty (2006b) however, observes that this final phase of 'Informed Professionalism' has never materialized due to the failure of phase three.

New Labour: A New Professionalism

As early as 1997, Whitty and Mortimore had indeed predicted the outcome of the reforms to be embarked upon by New Labour and had warned particularly against the continuing tendency to blame teachers that had begun in the early 1980s. Yet, the ensuing reforms were a response to this perceived failure by teachers to deal successfully with society's ills (Whitty, 2006b). New Labour's education policies were designed to modernize and transform all aspects of the education system and the teaching profession was no exception. In 1998, it launched a Green Paper – *Teachers: meeting the challenge of change* in which it set out its proposals for the 'most fundamental reform of the teaching profession since state education began' (DfES, 1998 cited in Furlong, 2008, p. 728). The Government's concerns about the teaching profession were numerous and many were longstanding (see Furlong, 2008 and Whitty, 2006c). They considered the 'Old Professionalism' that emphasized status based on years of service and exclusivity to be outdated and so, while addressing these concerns, the Government also sought to transform the teaching profession and to bring about a 'New Professionalism' one they considered more relevant to teaching in the twenty-first century (Furlong, 2008; Storey, 2009). This was to be achieved, according to Furlong (2008) through a series of measures aimed at:

- Make teaching a more attractive career in order to improve the supply and retention of good quality teachers
- Reforming the workforce and working practices in schools to facilitate teachers working in partnership with others in the school and to also offer them greater flexibility and career progression
- Reforming teacher professional development (CPD), to make it more school based and to ensure that there was a strong evidential base for any changes in practice - so called 'Extended Professionalism'(see Trowler, 2003, p. 22)
- Making teachers far more accountable, not only to their schools but also to parents, pupils, the wider community and, more importantly, to the government.

According to Storey (2009, p. 4), this 'New Professionalism' was 'about an exchange' – by accepting the proposed reforms the Government offered, teachers were given more 'rights' . . . an assurance of rewards for success for high performers in the classroom as well as in formal leadership positions; career-stage promotion opportunities within a structured framework, and professional development to underpin this. In addressing these concerns and in the name of raising standards, the New Labour Government, therefore, put in place a series of measures to facilitate the transformation of the profession which resulted in new forms of training, new working practices, new workers in the classroom and a new language of performance and appraisal (Ball, 2008). This included:

- Changes to teacher education (see below)
- Better pay but also performance related pay – an end to national pay bargaining with the establishment of the School Teachers' Review Body to advise on pay and conditions, bursaries to attract trainees to shortage subject areas like maths and science and the potential for teachers to be rewarded with higher salaries for skills and experience by passing the 'threshold' or by becoming an 'Excellent ' or 'Advanced Skills Teacher (AST)
- More opportunities for promotion – an emphasis on school leadership with the establishment of the National College and Fast Track Teaching Programmes to encourage teachers to take up leadership roles
- 'Workforce remodelling' – providing teachers with more time to prepare lessons and also more 'help' in the classroom. This involved the de-regulation of teaching to allow non-teaching staff to undertake activities that had previously been the 'exclusive' domain of the teacher e.g. Higher Level Teaching Assistants undertaking teaching activities. A more 'collaborative professionalism' was suggested with teachers working together and with others

- The Every Child Matters agenda which introduced a range of *other professionals* into the classroom setting, removing again some of the autonomy of the teacher. ECM introduced the notion of 'inter-professional' working and also provided an opportunity for teachers, and other professionals working with young children, to conceive their practice and role in a 'multi-professional' context in which the traditional excluding barriers of role, code and practice are removed. In addition, ECM also introduced new ways of teachers engaging with the wider community e.g. through the extended schools initiative
- A more 'managed professionalism' – with the government taking control over teachers' working lives by ensuring a direct alignment of professional goals and standards with government policy through the use of government targets based on national testing, national strategies with national training to facilitate compliance, professional standards, continuing professional development linked to targets and standards, constant appraisal, observation of practice, individual targets and performance related pay – making education a profession governed by the highest surveillance and accountable. (George and Clay, 2008)

The Impact of Policy on Teaching

Since Margaret Thatcher's government, there has been a constant attack on the professional autonomy of teachers that has had enormous impact on teachers' views of themselves and their approach to their role in society. This has been a direct result of a combination of devolution on the one hand, competition between schools and increased surveillance, all of which have operated to bring the profession under total control. Such a focus on more centralized prescription and a culture of performativity are not confined to the UK but, in fact, are global patterns in education policy. The effects may have been an increase in standards overall but these have not been accompanied by the promised increases in equality for the poorest children (Kelly, 2005 in Whitty, 2006b). This has led to an inevitable contradiction in policy whereby schools are apparently given greater freedom while the state retains total control of educational outputs in the form of test results, league tables, Ofsted inspections and even the standards students must demonstrate in order to become a qualified teacher.

Moreover, parents have been manipulated into believing in government targets according to Whitty (2006b) and help to uphold the government agenda by making demands on schools. This relates to the notion of stakeholders who have an interest in education, as a publicly funded phenomenon and continues New Labour's move away from the focus on teachers' skills to a principle of more collective responsibility which in itself, may not be entirely negative. However, it has been pursued in a manner that actually deskills teachers or 'de-professionalises' them. A generation of young teachers who have been told what to do, how to download lesson plans (see Chapter 6 on the Literacy Strategy) and how to follow national guidance on behaviour management may be incapable of defining their own role and may, in fact, accept their new status as merely that of a 'technician'.

Workforce remodelling has also, according to Thompson, 'undermined the professional status of teachers [and continues] to challenge both the serenity and the identity of teachers wherever and whenever there is pressure on resources' (2006, p. 199). She suggests, for example, that permitting Higher Level Teaching Assistants to take lessons devalues the professional training and knowledge base of the teacher. It also, she points out, denies the fact that the level of training and the knowledge base of the teacher is predicated on the notion that it will return the best outcomes for children and young people. Whitty (2006b), too, points out that having people without teaching qualifications left in total charge of classrooms, suggests that there is nothing special about teachers' professional expertise. Would we be as happy to have an operation performed by someone who had been on a short course in medical techniques? According to Gunter (2007), allowing others – bursars, technicians, classroom assistants etc. to carry out roles that have traditionally been undertaken by teachers, results in a struggle between teachers who wish to retain their traditional professional identity and privilege and the culture of business management that now pervades schools and which seeks to abandon old professional identities by opening them up to market forces in the name of flexibility and efficiency.

The focus too of the 'Professional Standards' (whichever version we consider) remains firmly on subject knowledge and classroom practice and also tends to 'marginalise professional knowledge and understanding which go beyond those limitations' (George and Clay, 2008, p. 107). Pickard and Powell (2005) comment on Early Years' colleagues' feelings that government has ignored the knowledge of a largely female workforce in favour of 'auditable skills,' while Hill (2007) poses the question of whether or not the much quoted emphasis on the 'reflective practitioner' is, in fact, just another form of self-surveillance? Finally, an inevitable effect of constant criticism and distrust has been the growing uncertainty teachers are experiencing about their own ability, identity and role in a twenty-first century education system.

Changing Identities

Teachers have always sought to question "what kind of teacher am I?" and "what kind of teacher do I want to be?" (Korthagen cited in Black, 2008, p. 4). Providing an answer to such questions has generated considerable research interest. One such study, the VITAE (Variations in Teachers' Work, Lives and Effectiveness Project: DfES 2001–2006) highlighted a number of conceptualizations or 'scenarios of being a teacher' (Day and Saunders, 2006, pp. 267–8):

- *The Ideal.* Teaching as service – wanting to make a difference
- *The Cynical.* Teaching as compliance to external designated standards and prescriptions
- *Reality.* Teachers as professionals, committed to making a difference and having to sustain that commitment against all odds and often at some personal expense
- *Sustained Commitment.* Teachers who are able to maintain their professional identity and commitment throughout the different phases of their career.

The findings of the VITAE study suggest that teachers with greater commitment and a greater sense of personal identity tend to be more effective teachers. The scenarios presented could also be interpreted as representing aspects of the contemporary teachers' potential 'lifecycle'. Many teachers enter the profession with an *idealistic* view of what it is to be a teacher – they want to make a difference, to have a positive effect on the lives of their pupils. They have either been inspired by good teachers or wish to address the poor teaching they encountered by becoming a good teacher themselves. Later, many teachers find, that in order to survive, they simply have to *comply* – the constant regimes of appraisal, testing, standards and inspections force them to conform and to mould their practice to suit the government's whim of the day, rather than to their own needs and those of the individual pupils whom they teach. For many teachers then, the *reality* of teaching becomes a subjugation of their own identity as a teacher which can result in stress and disillusionment and may eventually result in them leaving the profession.

Facing up to the reality of teaching and to disillusionment has inevitably led to an exodus of large numbers of teachers from the profession, interestingly, not from the 20+ age group but from those over 30 who were not trained under a standards agenda (Ross, 2000). Reasons cited for the decision to leave teaching often relate to school management systems, feeling unsupported by management in the face of an excessive workload and pupils' unreasonable behaviour. Many teachers move to jobs outside teaching where they feel they would be able to show more creativity and independent thinking; ironically both these aspects were previously thought to be part of the attraction of teaching as a profession (Ross, 2000). Ross also points out that this may be an indication that we are losing our most creative teachers.

The imposition of targets and performativity were also cited as having a negative impact on professional autonomy, while others seek to reconcile the dramatically different image of the teacher as technocrat with the teacher as instinctive and imaginative practitioner, causing a fracturing of identity. Interestingly, more men than women seem to be leaving the profession. Could this be, interpreted as women's greater ability to adapt, or, in fact, be evidence of their greater compliance?

Some teachers however, manage to *sustain their commitment* as a teacher by redefining themselves and thereby may avoid leaving the profession altogether. A study by Troman and Woods (2000) identified three strategies that were adopted by primary teachers who had all experienced sufficient stress to necessitate a career-break of some kind. The strategies were defined as *retreatism, downshifting* and *self-actualisation*. A number of studies have charted the dramatic increase in stress-related illness affecting teachers since 1988 and suggest that:

> Intensification leads to reduced time for relaxation and re-skilling, causes chronic and persistent work overload, reduces quality of service and separates the conceptualisation from the execution of tasks, making teachers dependent on outside expertise and reducing them to technicians. (Troman and Woods, 2000, p. 3)

Increased casualization of teaching, characterized by temporary and short-term contracts with increased reliance on supply teachers, especially in inner-city and challenging schools, has led many teachers to retreat to the position of abandoning ambition in favour of just being able to cope – 'What for some people had once been a vocation now became just a job' (ibid, p. 8). This was deemed to be a *retreating strategy*, that is, teachers were submitting to and accepting change as inevitable. Some decided to 'downshift' by accepting a reduced workload and demotion, while others sought to re-develop their identities by escaping altogether. Sometimes this might involve seeking out a school with values more similar to their own while others found greater satisfaction transferring to a job outside of teaching, yet, ironically, retaining their 'teacher identity' in that new locus of employment, taking on a nurturing or training role for colleagues. As Troman and Woods conclude, perhaps teaching is no longer a profession that should be embarked upon as a life-long commitment due to the emotional, physical and psychological demands of the job.

Focus on: Why teaching is not an attractive profession

Recruiting more 'high quality' graduates and well qualified 'career changers' into the teaching profession is one of the Government's priorities. As many assert, the quality of the education system is dependent upon the quality of its teachers. The low status of the profession (ranking alongside social work and nursing) together with low salaries and stressful working conditions are potential deterrents to many well qualified graduates, particularly those with degrees in maths, science, engineering and technology who can easily claim much higher salaries and better working conditions elsewhere. Such deterrents may outweigh the factors that generally attract people into teaching – a sense of vocation, a desire to 'give something back' and the opportunity to help others. In addition, there are more specific reasons why becoming a primary school teacher is not an attractive proposition for young males.

A report published in 2008 by the Policy Unit (see Freedman *et al.*, 2008) – an independent think tank, suggested the reasons why people are attracted to teaching and also why they do not find teaching an attractive career option. The table below highlights the top ten attractants and the top ten deterrents for graduates to entering the teaching profession as determined by the report:

Table 8.1 Top Ten Attractants and Deterrents to Undergraduates Entering the Teaching Profession

Top Ten Attractants	Top Ten Deterrents
• Long holidays	• Feeling unsafe in the classroom
• Helping young people to learn	• Salary
• Being inspired by a good teacher	• Working with children and young people
• Working with children and young people	• Teacher's morale
• Staying involved in a subject specialism	• The challenging nature of the job
• Giving something back to the community	• Having to handle parents
• The challenging nature of the job	• Concerns about how teachers and schools are inspected
• Wanting to be a better teacher than they experienced	• How the public perceives teachers/teaching
• Job security	• Speaking to teachers about the profession
• Fit with family or other commitments	• The professional status of teachers

Source: Freedman *et al.*, 2008, p. 16.

⇨

> **Focus on: Why teaching is not an attractive profession (cont'd)**
>
> Consider:
>
> - Why do you want to be a teacher? What do you find attractive about the role?
> - What makes being a teacher an unattractive career choice – is there anything that you would add to the list above?
> - Draw up a list of what you consider to be the benefits of having more male primary teachers and then a further list of the factors that might deter males from considering primary teaching as a career option. What do you think could be done to attract more males into primary teaching?

Teacher Education

Accredited teacher education and training courses have been central to raising the status of teaching as a profession. The 1960s heralded a massive expansion in the teaching workforce and also changes to teacher education programmes. First, existing Certificate programmes were lengthened to 3 years and then replaced with Bachelor of Education Degrees of 3 or 4 years duration, delivered by Higher Education Institutions. Such courses did much to define the nature of the profession and later, with the establishment of the Postgraduate Certificate in Education, helped to develop teaching as a graduate profession. As Gillard (2005, p. 176) highlights, in addition to 'school experience' such courses also included the study of the history and philosophy of education together with learning theory, psychology, child development and behaviour management. Later, in order to teach in a state school, a person also had to achieve Qualified Teacher Status (QTS). Over time, a variety of routes into teaching, currently numbering 32, have been developed. They include:

- Undergraduate teacher training routes – the BEd and BA/BSc routes with QTS
- Postgraduate teacher training – University based – Postgraduate certificate in education (PGCE) or School-centred initial teacher training (SCITT)
- Employment-based teacher training – the Graduate Teacher Programme (GTP), Registered Teacher Programme (RTP) and Teach First
- Assessment-based teacher training for individuals with substantial teaching experience but not QTS
- Overseas Trained Teacher Programme (OTTP).

Governments have always been suspicious of the role of Higher Education Institutions in the education of teachers. In the 1970s, for example, teacher trainers were held responsible for the failings of the education system and were blamed for 'inculcating generations of teachers with "woolly ideas" about equality at the expense of training teachers to teach the basic skills and to impart a fixed immutable body of knowledge' (George and Clay, 2008, p. 103). Successive governments have, therefore, sought to regain more control over the 'education' of teachers and to gradually move to more school based 'training'. Since 1979, both Conservative and New Labour Governments have pursued similar objectives with respect to teacher education. New Labour in particular saw initial teacher education as having a major role in the 're-tooling' of the teacher profession' (Furlong, 2008, p. 730). The reforms have included (see Ball, 2008 and George and Clay, 2008, pp. 107–8):

- *A change in emphasis* from 'education' to training. Teaching is now viewed more as 'craft' and training as an 'apprenticeship' in which competence is gained through observation and repetition of observed good practice.
- *A diversification of routes into teaching* – with 32 different routes into teaching, the system of teacher training in the UK is one of the most diverse in the world (Husbands, 2008).
- *The establishment of the Training and Development Agency for Teachers* (TDA) initially the Teacher Training Agency (TTA) a non-departmental, public body that oversees, manages and funds teacher training and also controls the supply of recruits into the profession.
- *The development of 'Partnership'* as a conceptual model for teacher training. Schools and higher education institutions now have to work together to deliver training, with schools now playing the central role. However, as Husbands (2008) observes the real, critical school–university partnerships that were desired have failed, on the whole, to emerge.
- *The introduction of centrally prescribed 'Professional Standards' for teachers*. The Standards have undergone a number of reviews since their inception and now include sets of standards for each stage in a teacher's career. The Standards apply to areas of teacher's knowledge and understanding, professional attributes and values and teaching. Some, like Ball, claim that the introduction of Standards 'finally eradicated the intellectual and disciplinary foundations of teacher education [replacing them with] . . . a skills and classroom management curriculum' (2008, p. 145).
- *The introduction of quality control in the form of Ofsted Inspections* – HEIs are regularly scrutinized and inspected to ensure that they comply with the centrally contrived standards. Student numbers are awarded to institutions on the basis of the 'quality' of their provision, so there is a pressure on providers to comply.
- *The development of fast routes into teaching, for example, Teach First* – a fast track, short training course for high quality graduates.

The Government's policy regarding teacher education has, according to Husbands (2008, p. 5), two main policy objectives which are to:

- Control the supply of 'quality' teachers
- Ensure the effective delivery of the National Curriculum and other national educational priorities.

In order to achieve this the Government have exercised considerable control over the process of Initial Teacher Education/Training. According to Husbands this has resulted in Initial Teacher Trainers being under 'intermittent, if occasionally ferocious attack' (2008, p. 7). He goes on to suggest that with New Labour 'an activist government pushing on with radical change meant that most teacher educators were *forced* to be reactive' (ibid.). As a consequence, Husbands suggests, that while there has been considerable government led innovation in terms of pedagogy (National Strategies), collaborative working (ECM) and the introduction of new technologies into the classroom, universities, surprisingly, have not played a central role in such innovations, in fact, he suggests that 'it is difficult to identify a sustained innovation which has emerged from within the ITE structure over the last decade' (ibid.). This degree of 'risk aversion' in ITE is becoming a policy concern, however, it is also, as Husbands suggests, paradoxical:

> ITE has been a conduit for the management of change at a time of rapid policy and practice change in education, but it has largely been centrally managed and directed change. (ibid., p. 7)

The notion of 'Partnership' has also proved problematic. According to Husbands, the rationale for more school-based training came from the work of McIntyre (2007) who suggested that schools provide the 'locus for the professional craft knowledge of teaching' while universities have access both to this craft knowledge and also to the evidence on which such school practice was based (2008, p. 4). However, although schools have been given the lead role in the training partnership, they have often been a reluctant partner, slow to take up their lead role and happy, even with employment based routes, to relinquish their responsibility to universities (Husbands, 2008).

The focus on 'professional craft knowledge' is also problematic and according to Wrigley, results in a 'contradiction at the heart of teacher education' so that training is 'torn between the poles of imitative apprenticeship and initiation into reflective practice' (2006, p. 297). Wrigley suggests that while teachers need initiation into school practices – to observe more experienced teachers, to experience the practice of teaching, they also need to be able to critically reflect on those experiences in a meaningful way. Indeed an 'imitative apprenticeship' should not be pursued at the expense of providing future teachers with an opportunity to explore the intellectual and ideological aspects of their practice. As Wrigley comments:

> Because the world is changing so dramatically and even the planet from which we drink and on which we draw breath seems increasingly precarious, we cannot evaluate schooling to how closely it approximates to the National Curriculum. The entire discourse of standardisation is radically out of tune with the challenges young teachers face . . . it would criminally irresponsible simply to 'train' new teachers to follow orders, so that they can foist uncritical attitudes onto another generation of young people in schools. (2006, pp. 303–4)

So Where Next with Teacher Education or Training?

As we have seen, the consequences of the reforms of teacher education have resulted in a focus on school-based training, rather than a university education. As Gillard points out:

> Most student teachers now have less than a year's training and are taught little or nothing about the history, philosophy or politics of education, child development, the relationship between

intelligence and ability, the influences on educational achievement, theories about how the brain handles information or behaviour management techniques. (2005, p. 178)

Most teacher trainers would, we feel, suggest a return to a more balanced form of 'education' for teachers. Such an education would obviously have a focus on practice and the observation and imitation of good practice but would also reclaim a more professional orientation at the expense of the current obsession with the tick box approach to standards and the collection of endless files of evidence in order to 'prove' that those standards have been achieved. It appears, however, from the information that is emerging from the new Coalition Government that a return to the halcyon days of teacher education will not be possible and that such a balanced education may never be realized. As Michael Gove, the Secretary of State for Education, highlighted in his speech to the National College soon after taking up office, his is a very different vision of the future:

> . . . we will reform teacher training to shift trainee teachers out of college and into the classroom. We will end the arbitrary bureaucratic rule which limits how many teachers can be trained in schools, shift resources so that more heads can train teachers in their own schools, and make it easier for people to shift in mid-career into teaching. Teaching is a craft and it is best learnt as an apprentice observing a master craftsman or woman. Watching others, and being rigorously observed yourself as you develop, is the best route to acquiring mastery in the classroom . . . Nothing should get in the way of making sure we have the best possible cadre of professionals ready to inspire the next generation. (2010, n.p.)

Summary – Redefining Teacher Professionalism

Whitty (2006b) argues that all is not lost for the teaching profession and that some of the reforms may indeed actually enhance professionalism. He refers to three stages in the process of this redefinition of teacher professionalism, with the first being an inevitable and desirable move away from outmoded constructs of the professional with its emphasis on elitism and 'secret' knowledge. Whitty also acknowledges New Labour's attempt to reconstruct an identity for teachers in a managerialist model which some teachers have grappled with, and what is refered to as the 'entrepreneurial identity' (Sachs, 1999 cited in Hill, 2007, p. 9). However, Whitty (2006b) also puts forward the notion of a further reconstruction based on the possibility of a new kind of partnership with parents and pupils, which results in a more collaborative and reflective practice that he calls a 'democratisation of professionalism'. It is indeed ironic that through the creation of the General Teaching Council, the Labour government might have bestowed on teachers the status of professional in a traditional sense. However, Whitty argues that teachers do not need to cling to an out-dated and exclusionary notion of their professionalism in order to defend their position.

Whitty is not the only researcher to call for a new form of collaboration between teachers and their communities, including those marginalized groups often at greatest risk. As Mahony and Hextall had recognized 'social inequalities both impinge on teachers and are to some extent reconstituted or challenged by them' (1997, p. 141) while 'It is vital that we educate future teachers to see the connections between schooling, education and the wider society' (George and Clay, 2008, p. 110). Others suggest that a 'redefined professionalism' is an 'imperative' for teachers, particularly in the context of globalization. They suggest that such a form of professionalism would be:

> . . . manifested in the qualities that require teachers to value and sustain the intellect, to work collaboratively with other stakeholders in education, to be responsible and accountable and to be committed to lifelong learning and reflexivity. (Gopinathan *et al.*, 2009, p. 36)

Gill and Pryor (2006, p. 286) observe that 'the construction of teachers' professional identity is often inextricable from their sense of self' and they present a model of professional development that is not dictated by government agendas, restricted to the prescription of 'good practice' or the cognitive domain. Teachers, they suggest, need to be given opportunities to 'question and rearticulate their assumptions, values and beliefs, their pedagogical underpinnings and educational visions' (ibid., p. 293). This reflects Sachs' notion of the 'activist identity' for teachers who are willing to collaborate in new partnerships to help realize specific projects in a changing community of practice (Whitty, 2006b, p. 14). Hargreaves, as long ago as 1994, had commented that at the heart of the community lies the potential for a new professionalism (Hargreaves, 1994 cited in Gill and Pryor, 2006, p. 294).

Teachers, therefore, have to overcome their low morale and the public has to learn to trust them again if we are to be able to see education as more than just a cognitive enterprise. They need to re-position themselves as enablers to take forward the goal of education as encouraging a holistic experience, which leads to the development of each individual's full potential. In such a way, we can engineer 'a shift from seeing teachers' professional learning as acquiring knowledge and skills to exploring the question of what it means to become a teacher' (Gill and Pryor, 2006, p. 291).

Useful References

Ball, S. J. (2008), *The Education Debate*. Bristol: Policy Press.

Galton, M. and MacBeath, J. (2008), *Teachers Under Pressure*. London: Sage.

Useful Websites

www.tda.gov.uk/teachers.aspx The Training and Development Agency website.

www.teachernet.gov.uk The education site for teachers and school managers.

www.tes.co.uk The Times Educational Supplement online resources for teachers.

www.radicalteacher.org An independent magazine for educational workers.

References

Addison, P. (1994), *The Road to 1945: British Politics and the Second World War.* London: Pimlico.

Ainsley, S., Foster, R., Groves, J., Grime, K. and Woolhouse, C. (2007), '"Making Children Count": issues and challenges facing schools in implementing the "Every Child Matters" Agenda'. Draft paper presented at the British Educational Research Association (BERA) Conference, Institute of Education, University of London, 5–8 September.

Alderson, P. (2007), 'Childhood, Youth and the Economy'. *Soundings*, 35, 115–26.

Alexander, R. (2008), 'The primary review: emerging perspectives on childhood'. Keynote lecture presented at the Conference on Childhood, Wellbeing and Primary Education, Central Hall, Westminster, March 2008. Available at: www.primaryreview.org.uk/Downloads/Childhood__Well-being_and_Primary_Education_Robin_Alexander_lecture_170308.pdf [10 July 2010].

— (2009), *Children, Their world, Their Education: Final Report and Recommendations of the Cambridge Primary Review.* London: Routledge.

Allen, M. (2007), 'Learning for Labour: specialist diplomas and14–19 education'. *Forum,* 49, (3), 299–304.

Allen, R. (2010), 'Does school autonomy improve educational outcomes? Judging the performance of Foundation Schools in England'. (DoQSS Working Paper No 1002.) February 2010. IOE London. 33 pages. Available at: www.repec.ioe.ac.uk/REPEc/pdf/qsswp1002.pdf [20 August 2010].

Allport, G. W. (1979), *The Nature of Prejudice.* Cambridge, MA: Perseus Books.

Anning, A. (2006), 'Early years education: mixed messages and conflicts', in D. Kassem, E. Mufti and J. Robinson (eds), *Education Studies: Issues and Critical Perspectives.* Berkshire: Open University Press, pp. 5–17.

Arnove, R. F. (2007), 'Introduction: reframing comparative education: the dialectic of the global and the local', in R. F. Arnove and C. A. Torres (eds), *Comparative Education: The Dialectic of the Global and the Local,* 3rd edn. Lanham, MD: Rowman & Littlefield, pp. 1–20.

Artiles, A. J., Harris-Murri, N. and Rostenberg, D. (2009), 'Inclusion as social justice: critical notes on discourses, assumptions, and the road ahead', in P. Hick and G. Thomas (eds), *Inclusion and Diversity in Education,* Vol 1. London: Sage.

Association of Teachers and Lecturers (ATL). (2008), *New Professionalism.* Available at: www.askatl.org.uk/atl [29 January 2009].

Baker, M. (2009), 'Crunch time for the diplomas: will they survive?' *Forum,* 51, (1), 85–91.

Baldock, P., Fitzgerald, D. and Kay, J. (2009), *Understanding Early Years Policy.* London: Sage.

Ball, S. J. (2003), 'The teacher's soul and the terrors of performativity'. *Journal of Education Policy,*18, (2), 215–28.

— (2006), *Education Policy and Social Class. The Selected Works of Stephen. J. Ball.* Oxon: Routledge.

— (2007), 'Choice, ethics and professional change in education markets. Full research report'. (ESRC End of Award Report. RES-000-27-0090). Swindon: ESRC.

— (2008), *The Education Debate.* Bristol: The Policy Press.

— (2009), 'Academies in context: politics, business and philanthropy and heterarchical governance'. *Management in Education,* 23, (3), 100–3.

Ball, S. J. and Vincent, C. (2005), 'The "childcare champion"? New Labour, social justice and the childcare market'. *British Educational Research Journal,* 31, (5), 557–70.

Ballantine, J. H. and Spade, J. Z. (2008), *Schools and Society: A Sociological Approach to Education.* Los Angeles: Pine Forge Press.

Barron, I., Holmes, R., Maclure, M. and Runswick-Cole, K. (2007), *Primary Schools and Other Agencies.* (Primary Review Research Survey 8/2). Cambridge: University of Cambridge Faculty of Education.

Bartlett, S. and Burton, D. (2007), *Introduction to Education Studies.* London: Sage.

Bates, J. E. and Lewis, S. E. (2009), *The Study of Education: An Introduction.* London: Continuum.

Beckett, F. (2008), 'Further reflections on the great city academy fraud'. *Forum,* 50, (1), 5–10.

Beckmann, A. and Cooper, C. (2004), '"Globalisation", the new managerialism and education: rethinking the purpose of education in Britain'. *Journal for Critical Education Policy Studies,* 2, (2), 13 pages. Available at: www.jceps.com/?pageI D+article&articleID=31 [26 June 2010].

Ben–Porath, S. R. (2009), 'School choice as a bounded ideal'. *Journal of Philosophy of Education,* 43, (4), 527–44.

Benn, M. (2006), 'Diversity and choice: the spin doctor's route to selection'. *Forum,* 48, (1), 9–12.

Bingham, J. (2009), '"Nappy curriculum" forces thousands of childminders to quit'. *The Telegraph.* 26 December. Available at: www.telegraph.co.uk/education/6885075/Nappy-curriculum-forces-thousands-of-childminders-to-quit-Tories.html [12 January 2010].

Bishopsgate Institute, Newspaper Cuttings File: City Press, 26 December 1874. Address by William Rogers at School Prize Giving.

Black, K. (2008), 'Who am I as a Teacher? the changing professional identity of teachers and the "Every Child Matters" agenda'. Paper presented at the Educational Effectiveness and Improvement SIG at the British Educational Research Association Annual Conference, Herriot-Watt University, Edinburgh, 3–6 September. Available at: www.beraconfer-ence.co.uk/downloads/BERA%202010%20web%202.pdf [4 October 2009].

Bondi, L. (1991), 'Choice and diversity in school education: comparing developments in the United Kingdom and the USA'. *Comparative Education,* 27, (2), 125–34.

Brandsma, J. (2002), 'Social exclusion and equality in education. new perspectives for learning'. (Briefing Paper 41). Available at: www.pjb.co.uk/npl/index.htm [2 May 2010].

Brannen, J. and Moss, P. (eds). (2003), *Rethinking Children's Care.* Buckingham: Open University Press.

Branson, N. (1975), *Britain in the Nineteen Twenties.* London: Weidenfeld and Nicolson.

Broadfoot, P. (2007), *An Introduction to Assessment.* London: Continuum.

Bull, B. (2009), 'Policy implications of social justice in education'. *Ethics and Education,* 4, (2), 141–52.

Butters, J. (n.d.), 'Teacher voice in educational policy making', Texas State University. Available at: www.txstate.edu/edphd/PDF/teachvoice.pdf. [10 January 2010].

Caldwell, B. J. (2007), 'School based management'. (Education Policy Series, International Academy of Education). Available at: http://unesdoc.unesco.org/images/0014/001410/141025e.pdf [3 June 2010].

Callaghan, D. (2006), *Conservative Party Education Policies, 1979–1997: The Influence of Politics and Personality.* Brighton: Sussex Academic Press.

Carlile, A. (2009), 'Sexism and permanent exclusion from school'. *Forum,* 51, (3), 333–42.

Chitty, C. (2008), 'The UK National Curriculum: an historical perspective'. *Forum,* 50, (3), 343–7.

— (2009), *Education Policy in Britain,* 2nd edn. Basingstoke: Palgrave Macmillan.

Cohen, B., Moss, P., Petrie, P. and Wallace, J. (2004), *A New Deal for Children?* Bristol: The Policy Press.

Coldron, J. (2007), 'Parents and the diversity of secondary education: a discussion paper'. Prepared for R.I.S.E, Centre for Education Research and Social Inclusion, Sheffield Hallam University, 27 pages. Available at: www.risetrust.org.uk/Diversity.pdf *[2 November 2009].*

Coles, J. (2006), Fault lines in New Labour's education project: points for intervention and resistance'. *Forum,* 48, (1), 13–22.

Curtis, A. (2009), 'Academies and school diversity'. *Management in Education,* 23, (3), 113–117.

Dainton, S. (2005), 'Reclaiming teachers' voices'. *Forum*, 47, (2, 3), 159–68.

Da Roit, B. and Sabatinelli, S. (2007), 'The cost of childcare in EU countries. Transversal analysis'. Part 1 of 2. (Study for the European Parliament's Employment and Social Affairs Committee). Available at: www.europarl.europa.eu/activities/committees/ . . . /download.do?file [2 December 2009].

Davies, M. (2005), 'Less is more: the move to person-centred, human scale education'. *Forum*, 47, (2, 3), 97–118.

Day, C. and Saunders, L. (2006), 'What being a teacher (really) means'. Forum (Special Issue). 48, (2), 265–74.

DePalma, R. and Atkinson, E. (2009), '"No outsiders": moving beyond a discourse of tolerance to challenge heteronormativity in primary schools'. *British Educational Research Journal*, 35, (6), 837–55.

Department for Children, Schools and Families. (2009), 'The Children's Plan one year on: a progress report'. Nottingham: DCSF Publications. Available at: www.ttrb.ac.uk/ViewArticle2aspx?anchorld=17746&menu=1. [2 November 2010].

— (2010), 'Identifying components of attainment gaps'. Available at: www.dcsf.gov.uk/research [10 July 2010].

Department for Education. (2010), 'What are free schools?'. Available at: www.education.gov.uk/freeschools/whatarefree-schools [18 July 2010].

Department for Education and Science. (2003), *Every Child Matters: a green paper*. London: DfES.

— (2005), *Youth Matters: summary*. Nottingham: DfES Publications.

Dyson, A. (2009), 'Beyond the school gate: schools, communities and social justice'. Paper presented at the British Educational Research Association Annual Conference, University of Manchester, 2–5 September 2009. Published in 2008 in *Orbis Scholae*, 2, (2), 39–54.

Eaglesham, E. J. R. (1967), *The Foundations of Twentieth Century education in England*. London: Routledge and Kegan Paul.

Edwards, T. (2002), 'Restructuring educational opportunity in England'. *Australian Journal of Education*, 46, (2), 109–20.

Eisner, E. W. (2002), The kinds of schools we need. *Phi Delta Kappa*, April, 576–82.

Eurydice. (2007), 'School autonomy in England'. Report prepared by the Eurydice Unit for England, Wales and Northern Ireland, September 2007, 30 pages. Available at: www.eacea.ec.europa.eu/education/eurydice/ . . . reports/090EN.pdf [20 August 2010].

Exley, S. and Ball, S. J. (2010), 'Something old, something new . . . understanding Conservative education policy'. Institute of Education, London. Available at: www.social-policy.org.uk/lincoln/ball_exley.pdf [26 July 2010].

Fisher, T. (2008), 'The era of centralisation: the 1988 Education Reform Act and its consequences'. *Forum*, 50, (2), 255–61.

Freedman, S., Lipson, B. and Hargreaves, D. (2008), 'More good teachers'. Policy Exchange. Available at: www.policyexchange.org.uk [20 June 2010].

Frost, N. and Parton, N. (2009), *Understanding Children's Social Care: Politics, Policy and Practice*. London: Sage.

Furlong, J. (2002), 'Ideology and reform in teacher education: some reflections on Cochran-Smith and Fries'. *Educational Researcher*, 31, (6), 23–35.

— (2008), 'Making teaching a 21st century profession: Tony Blair's big prize'. *Oxford Review of Education*, 34, (6), 727–39.

Gaine, C. and George, R. (1999), '*Gender, "Race" and Class in Schooling. A New Introduction*'. London: Falmer Press.

George, R. and Clay, J. (2008), 'Reforming teachers and uncompromising "standards": implications for social justice in schools'. *Forum*, 50, (1), 103–11.

Gerwitz, S. and Ball, S. J. (2000), 'From "Welfarism" to "new managerialism": shifting discourses of school headship in the education market place'. *Discourse Studies in the Cultural Politics of Education*, 21, (3), 253–68.

Gibbons, S., Machin, S. and Silva, O. (2006–2007), 'The educational impact of parental choice and school competition'. *CenterPiece*, Winter, 6–8.

Gill, S. and Pryor, J. (2006), 'The person who teaches? Narrative identity and teachers' experience at an international conference'. *Forum*, 48, (3), 285–96.

Gillard, D. (2005), 'Rescuing teacher professionalism'. *Forum,* 47, (2, 3), 175–80.

— (2007), 'Education in England: a brief history'. Available at: www.educationengland.org.uk/history [12 July 2010].

— (2008), 'Blair's academies: the story so far'. *Forum,* 50, (1), 11–22.

— (2010), 'Hobson's choice: education policies in the 2010 general election'. *Forum,* 52, (2), 135–44.

Gipps, C. (1993), 'The role of educational research in policy making in the UK'. Paper presented at the AERA Conference, Atlanta, Georgia, 12–16 April 1993.

Glatter, R. (2004), 'Choice and diversity of schooling provision: issues and evidence'. Memorandum to the Select Committee on Public Administration. Available at: www.parliament.uk [10 June 2010].

Goldring, E. B. and Phillips, K. J. R. (2008), 'Parent preference and parent choices: the public-private decision about school choice'. *Journal of Education Policy,* 23, (3), 209–30.

Goode, E. and Ben-Yehuda, N. (2009), *Moral Panics and the Social Construction of Deviance,* 2nd edn. Oxford: Wiley-Blackwell.

Gopinathan, S., Tan, S., Yan Ping, F., Devi, L., Ramos, C. and Chao, E. (2009), 'Transforming 21st century teacher education through redefined professionalism, alternative pathways and genuine partnership'. A report produced by the International Alliance of Leading Education Institutes.

Gove, M. (2010), 'Speech to the National College Annual Conference'. Birmingham 17 June. Available at: www.education.gov.uk/news/speeches/nationalcollegeannualconference [10 August 2010].

Gronn, P. (2000), 'Distributed properties: A new architecture for leadership'. *Educational Management & Administration.* 28, (3), 317–8l.

Gunter, H. (2007), 'Remodelling the school workforce in England: a study in tyranny'. *Journal for Critical Education Policy Studies,* 5, 1. Available at: www.jceps.com/?pageID=article&articleID=84 [22 May 2010].

Gutman, L. M., Brown, J. and Akerman, R. (2009), 'Nurturing parenting capability: the early years'. (Wider Benefits of Learning: Research Report 30). University of London, Institute of Education.

Hadden, R. (1888), *Reminiscences of William Rogers, Rector of St. Botolph.* London: Bishopsgate.

Hansen, A. (2009), 'Researching "teachers in the news": the portrayal of teachers in the British national and regional press'. *Education 3–13,* 37, (4), 335–47.

Hassan, N. (2009), 'Race and education', in J. Sharp, S. Ward and L. Hankin (eds), *Education studies. An issues-based approach,* 2nd edn. Exeter: Learning Matters.

Hatcher, R. (2008), 'England: new forms of management and governance in the school system in England'. Education in Europe: Analysis, Alternatives, Action. Available at: www.educationineurope.org.uk/spip.php?article6 [15 July 2010].

Hill, D. (2001), 'The third way in Britain. New Labour's neo-liberal education policy'. Paper presented at the Congres Marx International III, Le Capital et L'humanité, University of Paris, Nantes-Sorbonne, 26–29 September.

Hill, Y. (2007), 'Literature review on teacher professionalism'. (Unpublished doctoral dissertation). Keele University.

Hirsch, D. (2002), 'What works in innovation in education. School: a choice of directions'. (A CERI Working Paper). May 2002. Available at: www.oecd.org/dataoecd/21/0/2755749.pdf [15 July 2010].

Hobsbawm, E. (1998), *Uncommon People: Resistance, Rebellion and Jazz.* London: Abacus.

Humphries, S. (1981), *Hooligans or Rebels: Oral history of Working Class Childhood 1889–1939.* Oxford: Blackwell.

Hurt, J. (1972), *Education in Evolution.* London: Paladin.

Husbands, C. (2008), 'Reflections on issues in teacher education'. A report for the International Alliance of Leading Education Institutes. Available at: http://docs.google.com/viewer?a=v&q=cache:mTSPAMXzDecJ:www.intlalliance.org/UK.pdf+Husbands+reflections+on+issues+in+Teacher+Education [22 June 2010].

Jessop, B. (2003), 'From Thatcherism to New Labour: neo-liberalism, workfarism and labour market regulation'. Department of Sociology, Lancaster University. Available at: www.comp.lancs.ac.uk/sociology/soc131rj.pdf [2 December 2009].

Kamerman, S. B. (2006), 'A global history of early childhood education and care'. Paper commissioned for the Education for All Global Monitoring Report 2007: Strong foundations: early childhood care and education. Available at: www.unesdoc.unesco.org/images/0014/001474/147470e.pdf [31 October 2009].

Kassem, D., Mufti, E. and Robinson, J. (2006), *Education Studies: Issues and Critical Perspectives*. Berkshire: Oxford University Press.

Kelly, A. V. (2009), *The Curriculum Theory and Practice*, 6th edn. London: Sage.

Kirk, G. and Broadhead, P. (2007), 'Every Child Matters and teacher education: a UCET position paper'. (Occasional Paper No 17). Available at: www.ucet.co.uk [20 December 2009].

Lambeth Palace Library, Temple Papers, 1899 Home Vol 22. Letter from Vaughan Davies, 26 January 1899.

Laqueur, T. W. (1976), *Religion and respectability: Sunday schools and working class culture 1780–1850*. London: Yale University Press.

Larsen, T. P., Taylor-Gooby, P. and Kananen, J. (2006), 'New Labour's policy style: a mix of policy approaches'. *Journal of Social Policy*, 35, (4), 629–49.

Lawson, J. and Silver, H. (1973), *A Social History of Education*. London: Methuen.

Lawton, D. (2008), 'The National Curriculum since 1988: panacea or poisoned chalice?'. *Forum*, 50, (3), 337–41.

Leathwood, C. and Hayton, A. (2002), 'Educational inequalities in the United Kingdom: a critical analysis of the discourses and policies of New Labour'. *Australian Journal of Education*, 46, (2), 138–53.

Leaton Gray, S. (2006), 'What does it mean to be a teacher? Three tensions within contemporary teacher professionalism examined in terms of government policy and the knowledge economy'. *Forum*, 48, (3), 305–15.

Leckie, G. and Goldstein, H. (2009), 'The limitations of using school league tables to inform school choice'. CMPO Working Paper Series No 09/208). 1–20. Available at: www.bristol.ac.uk/cmpo [10th July 2010].

Le Métais, J. (1997), 'Values and aims in curriculum and assessment frameworks'. International Review of the Curriculum and Assessment Frameworks. March 1997. Available at: www.inca.org.uk/pdf/values_no_intro_97.pdf [10 December 2009].

Lister, R. (2006), 'Children (but not women) first: New Labour, child welfare and gender'. *Critical Social Policy*, 26, (2), 315–35.

Maclure S. J. (1973), *Educational Documents, England and Wales, 1816 to the Present Day*. London: Chapman and Hall.

Mahon, R. (2001), 'What kind of "Social Europe"? The example of child care'. Paper presented at the 1st IES Annual Colloquium The European Union: One Market, One Social Model? September 2001. (Working Paper No. 02/01). 28 pages. Available at: www.iee.umontreal.ca/publicationseng_fichiers/ . . . /Texte-Mahon01.pdf [7 October 2009].

Mahony, P. and Hextall, I. (1997), 'Sounds of silence: the social justice agenda of the Teacher Training Agency'. *International Studies in Sociology of Education*, 7, (2), 137–56.

Martin, D. (2009), 'A study of the development of the 21st century school. The quiet revolution'. Paper presented at the British Education Research Association New Researchers/Student Conference, University of Manchester. 2–5 September 2009, 1–5.

Marwick, A. (1970), *Britain in a Century of Total War: War, Peace and Social Change 1900–1967*. Harmondsworth: Penguin Books.

Matheson, D. (ed.). (2008), *An Introduction to the Study of Education*, 3rd edn. London: David Fulton.

McFall, J. (2009), 'The Treasury Select Committee – How it works, what it does, and its role in the Financial Crisis'. 9 October 2009. Available at: http://johnmcfall.com/news.aspx?i_PageID=109504 [20 January 2010].

McIntyre, E. (2009), 'Teacher discourse on lesbian, gay and bisexual pupils in Scottish schools'. *Educational Psychology in Practice*, 25, (4), 301–14.

Melhuish, E. (2007), 'The role of research in the development of Sure Start', in E. Melhuish, B. Taggart, I. Siraj-Blatchford and P. Tymms, 'The impact of research on policy'. Bera Sig: Educational Research and Policy Making. Symposium 8719.

British Educational Research Association (BERA) Annual Conference, Institute of Education, University of London, 7 September.

Melhuish, E., Taggart, B., Siraj-Blatchford, I. and Tymms, P. (2007), 'The impact of research on policy'. Bera Sig: Educational Research and Policy Making. Symposium 8719. British Educational Research Association (BERA) Annual Conference, Institute of Education, University of London, 7 September.

Morrell, D. (2003), 'What is professionalism?'. *The Catholic Medical Quarterly*, February. Available at: www.catholicdoctors.org.uk [20 February 2007].

Moser, M. (2006), 'Primary school choice in a rural locale: a "right, good, local school"'. Paper presented at the British Educational Research Association Annual Conference, University of Warwick, 6–9 September 2006.

Moss, P. (2003), 'Getting beyond childcare: reflections on recent policy and future possibilities', in J. Brannan and P. Moss (eds). (2003), *Rethinking Children's Care*. Buckingham: Open University Press, pp. 25–43.

— (2006), 'Farewell to childcare'. *National Institute Economic Review*, 195, January, 70–83.

Mowat, C. L. (1968), *Britain Between the Wars 1918–1940*. London: Methuen.

Mulderrig, J. (2002), 'Learning to labour: the discursive construction of social actors in New Labour's education policy'. University of Lancaster. Available at: www.ieps.org.uk/PDFs/dec02.pdf [10 June 2010].

Murphy, L., Mufti, E. and Kassem, D. (2008), *Education Studies: An Introduction*. Oxford: Oxford University Press.

Muschamp, Y., Wikeley, F., Ridge, T. and Balarin, M. (2007), *Parenting, Caring and Educating*. (Primary Review Research Survey 7/1). Cambridge: University of Cambridge Faculty of Education.

Nash, P. (2009), 'Let the witch-hunters eat cake'. Teacher Support Network. Available at: http://teachersupport.info/news/seced/the-15000-myth.php [3 February 2010].

Neal, S. and McLaughlin, G. (2009), 'Researching up? emotionality and policy making elites'. *Journal Social Policy*, 38, (4), 689–767.

Nichols, S., Nixon, H. and Rowsell, J. (2009), 'The "good" parent in relation to early childhood literacy: symbolic terrain and lived practice'. *Literacy*, 42, (2), 65–75.

Nixon, D. (2006), 'In praise of diversity: why schools should seek gay and lesbian teachers, and why it's still difficult'. *Forum*, 48, (3), 275–82.

Nutley, S. M., Davies, H. T. O. and Smith, P. C. (2004), *What Works? Evidence-based Policy and Practice in Public Service*. Bristol: The Policy Press.

OECD/CERI Secretariat. (2006), 'Parental choice and diversity of provision', in *Demand Sensitive Schooling*. Available at: www.oecd.org/document/11/0,3343,en_2649_39263231_37655499_1_1_1_1,00.html#HTO [15 July 2010].

Open Eye (2008), 'Early learning policies should not be imposed'. An open letter to the *Times*. 24 July 2008. Available at: www.timesonline.co.uk/tol/comment/letters/article4385896.ece [2 January 2010].

— (2010), 'The Open Eye campaign'. Available at: http://openeyecampaign.wordpress.com/about/ [2 January 2010].

Osgood, J. (2009), 'Childcare workforce reform in England and "the early years professional": a critical discourse analysis'. *Journal of Education Policy*, 24, (6), 733–51.

Overseas Development Institute. (2009), 'Evidence-based policy making'. Available at: www.odi.org.uk/Rapid/Projects/PPA0117/intro.html [3 January 2010].

Ozga, J. (1995), 'Deskilling a profession: professionalism, deprofessionalism and the new managerialism', in H. Busher and R. Saran (eds), *Managing Teachers as Professionals in Schools*. London: Kogan Page.

— (2004), 'From research to policy and practice: some issues in knowledge transfer'. *CES Briefings*, 31, April. Available at: www.ces.ed.ac.uk/PDF%20Files/Brief031.pdf [9 January 2010].

— (2009), 'Teacher professionalism quality assurance and evaluation'. (Presentation transcript). National Education Conference, 28 May 2009. Available at: www.slideshare.net/gtcs/teacher-professionalism-quality-assurance-and-evaluation-national-education-conference-28-may-2009 [20 July 2010].

Parekh, B. (2000), *The Future of Multi-Ethnic Britain – The Parekh Report*. London: Profile Books.

Parliamentary Papers. (1861), *Report of the Royal Commission Appointed to Inquire into the State of Popular Education in England*. The Newcastle Report.

— (1886), *Report of the Royal Commission on the Elementary Education Acts*. The Cross Report.

Parsons, C., Godfrey, R., Annan. G., Cornwall, J., Dussart, M., Hepburn, S., Howlett, K. and Wennerstrom, V. (2005), 'Minority ethnic exclusions and the race relations (amendment) act 2000'. Canterbury Christchurch College. Research Brief: RB616. February 2005. DfES.

Parton, N. (2009), 'From Seebohm to *Think Family*: reflections on 40 years of policy change of statutory children's social work in England'. *Child and Family Social Work*, 14, 68–78.

Patel, P. (2007), 'Every Child Matters: the challenge of gender, religion and multiculturalism'. *Forum*, 49, (3), 267–76.

Penn, H. (2007), 'Childcare Market Management: how the United Kingdom Government has reshaped its role in developing early childhood education and care'. *Contemporary Issues in Early Childhood*, 8, (3), 192–207.

Pickard, A. and Powell, J. (2005), 'Professionalism, multi-professionalism, inter-professionalism and trans-professionalism'. Paper delivered at the ATEE Conference, Amsterdam. Available at: www.ATEE2005.nl [10 February 2010].

Porter, J. (2009), 'Extravagant aims, distorted practice'. *Forum*, 51, (3), 289–98.

Powell-Davies, M. (2008), 'Haberdasher's Aske: the campaign against academies in Lewisham'. *Forum*, 50, (1), 61–70.

Precey, R. (2008), 'Trainspotting: leadership at a critical junction'. *Forum*, 50, (2), 235–42.

Pring, R. (2009), 'Education cannot compensate for society: reflections on the Nuffield Review of 14–19 education and training'. *Forum*, 51, (2), 197–204.

Prout, A. (2000), 'Children's participation: control and self-realisation in British late modernity'. *Children and Society*, 14, 304–15.

Public Record Office. *Granville Papers 30/29/21,* London.

Pugh, M. (1994), *State and Society: British Political and Social History 1870-1992*. London: Edward Arnold.

QCA. (2008), National Curriculum site. Available at: http://curriculum.qcda.gov.uk/ [10 December 2009].

Rea, J. and Weiner, G. (1997), 'Cultures of blame and redemption when empowerment becomes control: practitioner's views of the Effective Schools Movement'. Paper presented at the British Educational Research Association Annual Conference, University of York, 11–14 September 1997.

Richards, C. (2009), '"O Rose thou art sick", "O Testing, thou art malign": a critique of two official reports (with apologies to William Blake)'. *Forum*, 51, (3), 299–303.

Richardson, R. (2006), 'Playgrounds, the press and preventing racism: a case study'. *Forum*, 48, (2), 181–7.

Rikowski, G. (2003), 'The business takeover of schools'. *Mediactive*, 91–108.

Robertson, R. and White, K. E. (2003), *Globalisation: Critical Concepts in Sociology*. London: Routledge.

Roche, J. and Tucker, S. A. (2007), 'Every Child Matters "tinkering" or "reforming" – an analysis of the development of the Children's Act (2004), from an educational perspective'. *Education 3-13*, 35, (3), 213–23.

Rose, J. (2007), 'Multi-agency collaboration: a new theoretical model'. Paper presented at the British Educational Research Association (BERA) Conference, Institute of Education, University of London, 5–8 September.

— (2009), *Independent Review of the Primary Curriculum*. London: DCSF.

Ross, A. (n.d.), 'Some teachers' disillusionment with the profession'. Institute for Policy Studies in Education, University of North London. Available at: www.re-net.ac.uk/ . . . /eade599f-5fd9-4d73-92ae-8beb3c817848.doc [29 June 2010].

Rüling, A. (2008), 'Reframing of Childcare in Germany and England: From private responsibility to economic necessity'. *gsge Research Paper*. Available at: www.agf.org.uk/cms/upload/pdfs/WP/200810_WPcsge_e_re-framing_of_childcare. pdf [20 August 2010].

Sachs, J. (2003), 'Teacher professional standards: controlling or developing teaching?'. *Teachers and Teaching: Theory and Practice*, 9, (2), 175–86.

Savage, M. and Miles, A. (1994), *The Remaking of the British Working Class, 1840–1940*. London: Routledge.

Seaman, L. C. B. (1970), *Post-Victorian Britain 1902–1951*. London: Methuen.

Serf, J. (2008), 'Global learning in a changing and unpredictable world'. *Forum,* 50, (3), 411–18.

Simkins, T. (2000), 'Education reform and managerialism: comparing the experiences of schools and colleges'. *Journal of Education Policy,* 13, (3), 317–32.

Sinnott, S. (2008), 'Academies: a breakthrough or yet more spin?'. *Forum,* 50, (1), 41–8.

Smedts, G. (2008), 'Parenting in a technological age'. *Ethics and Education,* 3, (2), 121–34.

Smith, J. T. (2009), *A Victorian Class Conflict? Schoolteaching and the Parson, Priest and Minister 1837–1902*. Eastbourne: Sussex Academic Press.

Spielhofer, T., Golden, S., Evans, K., Marshall, H., Mundy, E., Pomati, M. and Styles, B. (2010), 'Barriers to participation in education and training'. (Research Briefing: DFE-RB 009). NFER.

Storey, A. (2009), 'How fares the New Professionalism in schools? Findings from the "State of the Nation" Project'. *Curriculum Journal,* 20, (2), 121–38.

Straker, K. and Foster, R. (2009), 'Every child matters: every challenge met?'. *Journal of Vocational Education and Training,* 61, (2), 119–32.

Sutton, R. (1999), *Working Paper 118: The Policy Process: An Overview*. Overseas Development Institute. London: Chameleon Press. Available at: www.odi.org.uk/resources/download/1868.pdf *[20 December 2009]*.

Taggart, B., Sylva, K., Melhuish, E., Siraj-Blatchford, I. and Sammons, P. (2007), 'Influencing policy through research on early childhood', in E. Melhuish, B. Taggart, I. Siraj-Blatchford and P. Tymms. (2007), 'The impact of research on policy'. Bera Sig: Educational Research and Policy Making. Symposium 8719. British Educational Research Association (BERA) Annual Conference, Institute of Education, University of London, 7 September.

Teacher Development Agency. (2008), 'Types of schools in England'. Available at: www.tda.gov.uk/teachers/overseas_trained_teachers/english_ed [16 September 2008].

Teachernet. (2009a), 'Extended Services'. Available at: www.teachernet.gov.uk/wholeschool/extendedschools/ [2 December 2010].

— (2009b), 'Early Years Foundation Stage (EYFS)'. Available at: www.teachernet.gov.uk/teachingandlearning/eyfs/ [5 December 2009].

Tett, L. (2008), 'Policy discourses and socially situated participation in education'. Paper presented at the 38th Annual SCUTREA Conference, University of Edinburgh, 2–4 July 2008.

Thompson, E. P. (1968), *The Making of the English Working Class*. London: Penguin.

Thompson, M. (2006), 'Re-modelling as de-professionalisation'. *Forum,* 48, (2), 189–200.

Titcombe, R. (2008), 'How academies threaten the comprehensive curriculum'. *Forum,* 50, (1), 49–58.

Tomlinson, S. (2005), *Education in a Post-Welfare Society*, 2nd edn. Berkshire: Oxford University Press.

Troman, G. and Woods, P. (2000), 'Careers under stress: teacher adaptations at a time of intensive reform'. Paper presented at the British Educational Research Conference, Cardiff University, September, pp. 1–26.

Tropp, A. (1957), *The School Teachers: The Growth of the Teaching Profession in England and Wales from 1800 to the Present Day*. London: Heinemann.

Trowler, P. (2003), *Education Policy. Gildredge Social Policy*, 2nd edn. London: Routledge.

Unicef. (2007), 'Child poverty in perspective: an overview of child well-being in rich countries'. Innocenti Report Card No 7. Available at: www.unicefirc.org/publications/pdf/rc7_eng.pdf [1 December 2009].

Wadsworth, J. and George, R. (2009). 'Choosing the right approach: New Labour and the care and education of young children. *Forum,* 51, (3), 309–18. http://dx.doi.org/10.2304/forum.2009.51.3.309

Ward, S. (ed.). (2008), *A Student's Guide to Education Studies*, 2nd edn. London: Routledge.

Ward, S. and Eden, C. (2009), *Key Issues in Education Policy*. London: Sage.

Warwick, I., Chase, E. and Aggleton, P. with Sanders, S. (2004), 'Homophobia, sexual orientation and schools: a case review and implications for action'. (Research Briefing: RB594). Institute of Education, University of London. November 2004. DfES.

Webb, R. K. (1969), *Modern England: From the 18th Century to the Present*. London: Allen and Unwin.

West, A. and Currie, P. (2008), 'School diversity and social justice: policy and politics'. *Educational Studies, 34*, (3), 241–50.

West, A. and Pennell, H. (2000), 'Publishing school examination results in England: incentives and consequences'. *Educational Studies, 26*, (4), 423–36.

West, A., Barham, E. and Hind, A. (2009), *Secondary Schools Admissions in England: Policy and Practice*. Education Research Group, London School of Economics and Political Science. Commissioned by R.I.S.E. with financial support from the Esmée Fairbairn Foundation. 50 pages. Available at: www.risetrust.org.uk/Secondary.pdf *[2 April 2009]*.

Whitty, G. (2002), *Making Sense of Education Policy*. London: Paul Chapman.

— (2006a), 'Education(al) research and education policy making: is conflict inevitable?'. *British Educational Research Journal, 32*, (2),159–76.

— (2006b), 'Teacher professionalism in a new era'. Paper presented at the first General Teaching Council for Northern Ireland Annual Lecture, Belfast, March 2006.

— (2006c), 'Teacher Professionalism. What Next?'. Kings College London: C-TRIP Seminar 9, 26 June 2006. Available at: www.kcl.ac.uk/content/1/c6/01/41/80/paper-whitty.pdf [20 November 2009].

Wilby, P. (2008), 'Education and social mobility'. *Forum, 50*, (3), 349–52.

Wilkin, A., White, R. and Kinder, K. (2003), *Towards Extended Schools: A Literature Review*. Research Report No 432. Nottingham: DfES Publications.

Wolf, A. (2002), *Does Education Matter? Myths About Education and Economic Growth*. London: Penguin.

Wrigley, T. (2006), '"Training" is just not good enough'. *Soundings, 48*, (3), 297304.

Yarker, P. (2009), '"This is determination": grass roots opposition to academies'. *Forum, 51*, (3), 319–22.

Yeo, A. and Lovell, T. (2002), *Sociology and Social Policy for the Early Years*. London: Hodder and Stoughton.

Youdall, D. (2008), 'Hidden privatisation in state education'. *The Australian Teacher*, Autumn, 16–17.

Index